C000192819

THE GIFTS
AND BAPTISM
OF THE SPIRIT

THE GIFTS AND BAPTISM OF THE SPIRIT

The manifestation of
the Spirit is given to every man
to profit withal

1 CORINTHIANS 12:7

JOHN METCALFE

THE PUBLISHING TRUST
CHURCH ROAD, TYLERS GREEN, PENN, BUCKINGHAMSHIRE

Printed and Published by
The John Metcalfe Publishing Trust
Church Road, Tylers Green
Penn, Buckinghamshire

–

Distributed by Trust Representatives
and Agents world-wide

In the Far East

Bethany, Orchard Point P.O. Box 0373
Singapore 912313

–

–

First Published 2001

–

ISBN 1 870039 80 7

–

**This work is available at less than the
cost of production through subsidies on
the part of the John Metcalfe Publishing
Trust. The Author waives all royalties in
favour of the Trust, a Registered Charity.**

CONTENTS

THE GIFTS
AND BAPTISM
OF THE SPIRIT

Introduction

BEFORE proceeding with this new – and corrective – passage in the First Epistle to the Corinthians – that is, Chapter 12:1-13 – it seems appropriate to remark on the consistent evangelical principles by which the apostle rectifies any and all deviations and errors on the part of the Corinthians; and, moreover, to notice with care that by which he does *not* correct them.

What do I mean by this, especially at such an advanced point in the epistle? I mean that for all the error, all the misconduct– one might even add despite certain riotous and lawless elements not only among them but tolerated by all of them – a most conspicuous feature appears in the apostle's response which it is of the utmost importance to note.

1

What is this? It is Paul's consistent appeal to the evangel of Christ.

Never once is the law brought in to correct the error. Not at all does the apostle appeal to the ten commandments to counter the deviation. No, not for any one thing. But this would most surely have been the case had those who framed the so-called Westminster Confession been at this business, or had those who insist on the law as 'a rule of life' addressed the conditions at Corinth.

Then how much more would the pallid and vitiated mimics of those Puritans – now calling themselves 'reformed': the impudence! – have set about wagging their pygmy legal fingers upon every occasion!

But what have any of these sterile deviates from the evangel, or the least part of their impotent legal court of appeal, to do with the matter? What? appeal to *the letter that killeth*, in order to restore to life? Paul *always* appeals to *the evangel of Christ*.

From which it is evident – and ought well to be noted – that such confounded legalists preach *another* gospel, and, I affirm, *another* Jesus, with *another* spirit, and have *another* ministry than that of the apostles of Christ, who handle everything upon an entirely different basis, namely, that of the evangel alone, by which deliverance from the law and the legal rule is for ever assured through the death of Christ.

I

The Spirit of God

IN I Corinthians 12:1 the apostle first comes to things spiritual. Not that such things had been neglected hitherto: indeed, in either verb or noun form, out of some twenty-six new testament references, fifteen of these occur in this epistle, of which I Corinthians 12:1 is the ninth.

This epistle contains far and away the greatest number of references to *pneumatikos*, whatever the precise grammatical form. And yet the Corinthians were not those whom one would have thought to be the most spiritual in practice!

The word *gifts*, as in spiritual *gifts*, I Corinthians 12:1, is nothing but interpolation. There is no precise English equivalent to the Greek. One might say literally 'spiritualities', but this does not at all cover the whole range of the Greek word. Other alternatives include 'things spiritual'; 'that which is spiritual'; and 'spiritual matters', but none of these quite does justice to the original.

3

However, the alternative renderings do make the idea perfectly clear.

Paul is to speak to the Corinthians, and correct them, over things that were spiritual. Regarding such things, he would not have them to be ignorant.

Nevertheless, from the past – in a more sinister context – there was that in this realm of which they certainly were *not* ignorant: 'Ye *know* that ye were Gentiles, *carried away* unto these dumb idols, even as *ye were led*', I Corinthians 12:2.

The idols were dumb, but that invisible spiritual power which carried them away to them was not dumb. The idols were dumb, they knew that, but willingly enough they followed those spirits that led them to them, and that knowingly: 'Ye know that.'

They knew that they were 'carried away', as men say, 'beside themselves', because of the licentious abandonment associated with idolatry, so that far from resisting they welcomed the heightened excitement which these animated spirits induced in their already eager lusts.

But they knew precisely what was happening when they were 'carried away'. Likewise when they 'were led'. They knew it was wrong. But they followed the inward urging within their passions, animated by the spirit that now worketh in the children of disobedience.

Why? Because by following these interior influences in their senses, they knew that the pitch of their excitement when taking part in the vile practices of idolatry would be far greater than if merely left to themselves. Hence they followed the spirit by which they 'were led', and they did so knowingly.

Today, the people are just as carried away in their pleasures, just as led in their excitements, but, unlike the Gentiles of old, they are utterly blind to the supernatural and demonic influences to which they give themselves up in order to fulfil their lusts.

But where did all this lead the Corinthians? Into idolatry, riotousness, fornication and drunkenness. But had not such wickedness been rebuked *among them still* in the earlier part of the epistle? Then to what spirit were such persons giving themselves over in the church – or *ecclesia* – of God?

Wherefore Paul gives them to understand what it is to be moved within, and led in the interior, by the Spirit of God. For they must never forget in their emotional excitement – or in that abandonment – to which they gave themselves so easily: *there were more spirits abroad to take advantage of such states than the Spirit of God.* Wherefore, 'believe not every spirit, but try the spirits whether they are of God', I John 4:1.

Negatively: 'No man speaking by the Spirit of God calleth Jesus *anathema*', I Corinthians 12:3. But whoever would do that? The legalists would, and did, and so did those who sought to bring back the law under the guise of a 'rule of life'.

They protest? It is the protest of liars: the Jesus they profess is another Jesus. But the Jesus they deny is the true Jesus. Then, by their Antinomian and unevangelical heresy – whosoever they are, it maketh no difference to me: God accepteth no man's person – *denying that Christ by his death lawfully delivered us not only from the penalty of the law, but also from the law itself, therefore they abhor, reject, and cry 'anathema' against such a Jesus as this, and such a lawful deliverance as the apostle enjoined.* Nevertheless *this* is the true Jesus.

Here is the very doctrine of Galatians; just as these same legal heretics are those exposed by II Corinthians 11:3,4 and 13-15. Denying Jesus *as he is in truth, outraged at the violation of their so-called 'systematic theology' by the reality of that redemption through which we have been set free from the law, being delivered by his death*

5

from the entire legal system for ever, they subtly reintroduce *another Jesus, which fictional character they pretend kept the law for us in his lifetime, yet brings us back into bondage under its—supposedly sanctionless!—legal rule for the rest of our lifetime.* Outraged at the very idea of any other *Jesus, namely, Jesus as he is in truth, with venomous fury they hiss at such a Redeemer so offensive to their legal system: 'anathema'.*

Then—I Corinthians 12:3—*they have not, and cannot have, the Spirit of God.* They have another, an opposing, a wholly different spirit. Read 'Justification by Faith'; and read 'Deliverance from the law: the Westminster Confession Exploded'. That is, if you would save yourselves from this untoward generation, and find the truth, as the truth is in Jesus.

Positively, no man can say that Jesus is the Lord—that is, say 'Lord Jesus'—but by the Holy Ghost. Men do not glorify him: the Spirit glorifies him. Men do not speak of him: they use his name to speak of themselves. Men do not submit to Jesus as Lord: they claim his name and power to lord it over others. O, it is not by might, nor by power, but by my Spirit, saith the Lord: *nothing* can be done aright but by him, and in him, and through him.

The Spirit of God has come to magnify the Lord Jesus: not to assist men in using his name to magnify themselves: 'He shall glorify me; he shall not speak of himself.' Then, how much less shall those whom he leads to say 'Lord Jesus', speak of *themselves?* The Spirit of truth always speaks of *him*, never of *himself*; always glorifies *him*, never *himself*; always leads to *him*, never to *himself*.

By this we know that Christ is always magnified and exalted by the Holy Ghost, who on the one hand safeguards from error, and whatever derogates from the Lord's glory, and on the other *always speaks of Christ, and upholds the doctrine of Christ, exulting and triumphing in those whom he indwells with the victorious exclamation from the heart:* 'Jesus is Lord!'

By this we know the Spirit of God.

6

II

The Gifts of the Spirit

SINCE this entire phase of the epistle is concerned with unity, the apostle now shows the unity of divine persons revealed in the new testament, yet, in this unity, divine activity, demonstrating the diversity of gifts, administrations, and operations respectively.

This diversity proceeds from each divine person revealed in the new testament, demonstrably manifesting the oneness of God in three persons through the revelation of Christ. Then how can the Corinthians possibly detach, say, gifts from the Giver; ministries from the Administrator; or operations from the Operator, setting these things at variance the one against the other, as if everything did not proceed from each divine person respectively, and as if divine persons were not one in the Godhead?

Yet this divine unity and united activity was what the Corinthians were denying in effect, particularly as they vied,

7

envied, and competed one against another in respect of their distinctive and differing gifts. Now this concerns spiritual things, brethren.

But all their spiritual gifts, however differing, *manifested the one person of the Holy Ghost*: 'But the manifestation of the Spirit is given to every man to *profit* withal': not to *contend* withal.

Gifts are to profit: not to divide; not to dissent; not to envy; not to argue; not to create schism. But *to manifest the Spirit*. That is, the making visible, with supernatural implications, *of what is otherwise unseen, namely, the unity of the Spirit.*

To make visible – manifest – what is invisible, namely, the presence of the divine Giver of the gifts, one in the Godhead with the Father and the Son. 'But all these worketh that one and the selfsame Spirit, dividing to every man severally as he will', I Corinthians 12:11.

Then what was this, that there were divisions among them, and contentions, to further which each separate party *used the gifts he had received to uphold his own particular sectarian position?*

What is it? It is schism, and of the worst sort, against the unity of the Spirit, and of the one body, contrary to him, and against themselves.

From the context, and the following passage on the body of Christ in the same chapter, it is evident that the gifts of which the apostle speaks are, first, from the Holy Ghost, and, second, within the body. The name that is given to such gifts is, singular, *charisma*, and, plural, *charismata*.

The *charismata* listed in I Corinthians 12:8-10 by no means indicates a fixed and inevitable series of gifts. The gifts may vary greatly from one *ecclesia* to another, and, judging by the apostle's injunction to 'covet earnestly the *best* gifts', I Corinthians 12:31, may even change from one gift to another within the same congregation.

Then, to presuppose either *fixed lists* or *inevitable gifts* is to superimpose the will of man and contradict the will of the Spirit who 'divideth to every man severally as *he* will', I Corinthians 12:11.

In the case of the *charismata* selected as an example by Paul in I Corinthians 12, it is well to note both the order and number of those given. Besides this, since he speaks of the 'best' gifts, it follows that these must be less than the total number listed; otherwise, were none better than another, there could be no 'best'.

Besides this, there appears an evident flexibility in the prospect of improving one's profitability to the whole body, by ascending from an inferior to a superior gift to profit, thus showing the Spirit's willingness to answer to a man's spiritual aspirations to the benefit of his brethren by the very best *charisma*.

Then, it would be crass ignorance to be bound by the letter— the *dead* letter—as opposed to the living Spirit indicated in I Corinthians 12:8-10.

What *is* certain, in the unity of the body of Christ, indwelt by the Holy Ghost, is that 'the manifestation of the Spirit is given to *every* man to profit withal', I Corinthians 12:7; that such a manifestation is at once spiritual, supernatural, and divine; and that the manifestation takes the form of various gifts bestowed by the one Spirit of God, as it is written, 'But all these worketh that one and the selfsame Spirit, dividing to every man severally as he will', I Corinthians 12:11.

If so, there is none without a gift, but all the gifts together in harmony make clear that there is one Spirit; one Lord; and one God and Father, who is above all, and through all, and in all. *That* is what the gifts—whatever they may be—are *for*, and it is *that* which the effectual working of every part makes manifest.

Then, this applies *only* in the body of Christ, *never* in a schism, or on a lesser, divided ground such as denominationalism.

Equally, it is impossible for it to apply where a hired so-called minister or priest takes the pre-eminence and does everything himself, the congregation remaining mute under his presumed ministrations.

Now consider the gifts mentioned by Paul in this place: First, the word of wisdom; second, the word of knowledge; third, faith; fourth, the gifts of healing; fifth, the working of miracles – literally, the inworkings of acts of power – sixth, prophecy; seventh, discerning of spirits; eighth, kinds of tongues; ninth, interpretation of tongues.

Oh? Where is the tenth? Mark my words, there is far, far more behind the choice of the apostle as to these *charismata* than appears on the surface, or on face-value to the superficial. Let would-be 'copiers' beware, and more than beware.

Now therefore carefully examine this ninefold list against the background already made manifest in this highly corrective epistle. Corrective, yes, but it is wonderful to behold the love of the apostle for his own children in the faith, and the care he lavishes upon them lest they should be overwhelmed by the rebukes which they richly deserved in so many areas.

Yet Paul finds occasion to praise them again and again, nor once does he lose heart despite the chaotic and erroneous depth of their fall. He never once forgets, or lets slip out of his mind, the calling and power of God put forth in their beginnings.

Such a remembrance enables him to say in the present tense what none but the eyes of one in the very spirit of I Corinthians 13 could possibly consider to be a realistic description of the state he sets out to correct.

But he remembers – and reminds them – full of the encouragement of love: 'I thank my God always on your behalf, for the grace of God which is given you by Jesus Christ; that in every thing ye are enriched by him, in all utterance, and in all knowledge; even as the testimony of Christ was confirmed in you: so that ye come behind in no gift; waiting for the coming of our Lord Jesus Christ: who shall also confirm you unto the end, that ye may be blameless in the day of our Lord Jesus Christ. God is faithful, by whom ye were called unto the fellowship of his Son Jesus Christ our Lord', I Corinthians 1:4-9.

Still, despite the love that beareth all things, believeth all things, hopeth all things, endureth all things, that never faileth, nevertheless all things must be corrected by the word of the truth of the evangel, and this the apostle fails not to bring home in due order to the *ecclesia* at Corinth.

First, to one is given by the Spirit the word of wisdom. That may have been so prior to their being led astray, and it may be so in theory, but in practice the apostle enquires, 'Is it so, that there is not a wise man among you?', I Corinthians 6:5.

There is about the nine *charismata* a kind of gentle – and unspoken – irony, which he who had eyes to see would have discerned.

For not only is the list of *charismata* in I Corinthians 12:7-11 an objective statement of general principles – as opposed to its being an account of what existed at that time in Corinth as a matter of fact – that is, it is general teaching, not historical record; but the apostle so selects and arranges the nine examples of *charisma* that the Corinthians – did they reflect upon it – might well perceive a hidden rebuke in the issue.

Is it the word of wisdom? Yet they had become enamoured with the wisdom of this world. But Christ, the wisdom of God in a mystery, had never been made known by the wisdom of the wise, which God had made foolish by the Cross. Christ was made known by the spiritual wisdom, even the hidden wisdom of God in a mystery, which stands in the gift of the Spirit.

Which *spiritual* wisdom was precisely what they lacked, not what they possessed. Read Chapters 1 to 12.

Or is it the word of knowledge? Well, both wisdom and knowledge were said to be in a word – the *word* of wisdom; the *word* of knowledge – and that word was the word of the truth of the evangel, the doctrine of Christ, whom the Spirit, the same Spirit, would glorify in the midst of the assembly by his own divine gifts.

This both magnified Christ, honoured the Father, and united the brethren. Now, brethren, where was that divinely given, spiritually conveyed word of wisdom, and word of knowledge, from that one and the selfsame Spirit, who should work such divine wonders among you, so unmistakably from God, indwelling the *ecclesia*, in Father, Son, and Holy Ghost?

Again, the Spirit gave faith, not man. It was not man's conjuring tricks in the letter and form, it was the power of God in the Holy Ghost. And whence came, and what was so evident from this divine manifestation of the Spirit? Why, that faith came by hearing, and hearing by the word of God. But what prevailed at Corinth? The apostolic word of God, or the contending voices of man?

Fourthly, gifts of healing. Note that this is in the plural. Well, so were their schisms, divisions, parties, contentions, and verbal conflicts that set one against another. These – being in the plural – needed *gifts* of healing, and many healings at that, before the body was made sound from its bruises and self-inflicted wounds.

Oh, *they* needed the gifts of healing most assuredly, who, failing to profit from the infallible word of wisdom by the Spirit, the incontestable word of knowledge – that is, of Christ by the same Spirit – were yet rent with *their* divisions and lacerating encounters. Was it not evident that they stood in such dire need of the healing of the Spirit, to bring them into the wholeness of unity by the gentleness and meekness of Christ, through the mystery of the gospel?

Fifth, 'working of miracles', declares the Authorized Version; but, more literally, this is 'the gift of inworking of acts of power'. How they needed *that*, in due sequence of wisdom, knowledge, faith, and healing, to prevent anew their abuse of external words and formal truths, that these might not again be carnally corrupted in and by their diverse mouths of contention, but inwrought by the power of God in the unity of the faith, and of the one and the selfsame Spirit.

O that thus their faith should not stand in the wisdom of men, but in the power of God; not in the dead letter which killeth, but in the quickening Spirit who giveth life.

But this cannot be without the *inworking* of acts of *power*, by which their *hearts* should be comforted, being knit together in love, and unto all riches of the full assurance of understanding, to the acknowledgement of the mystery of God, and of the Father, and of Christ. Thus all should be united *within* by the indwelling of God in Father, Son, and Holy Ghost. What a gift of grace *this* would be!

Next, prophecy. But had this *really* been among them, then surely the Spirit would have declared his being grieved; and, the inevitable future consequences of their unruly conversation and conduct having been foretold by the mouth of the prophet, they should surely have been shocked into repentance, and brought under the fear of God in mortification.

To another is given the *charisma* of discerning of spirits. But if *this* were so evident, and being exercised to the profit of all, how was it that the 'knowledgeable' took meat at the idols' temples, or else knowingly bought it in the shambles, since those with whom they went to such feasts 'were Gentiles, *carried away* unto these dumb idols, even *as they were led*', I Corinthians 12:2?

13

Did such a *charisma* as discerning of spirits exist at Corinth, then would no warning sound, no plea of love for the weak brother, have arisen in their midst? Were this gift in evidence, how then should it have fallen to the absent apostle to expostulate, 'Concerning *spirituality*, brethren, I would *not* have you to be ignorant', I Corinthians 12:1?

Had this gift been in evidence, and exercised, they would *not* have been ignorant. And yet still the resource was in that one and the selfsame Spirit, brethren: then whence and why the lack?

Next – and eighth – Paul mentions the Spirit giving to another divers kinds of tongues. Well, the Spirit *may* bestow such a gift, to speak in terms of general principle; or in terms of objective teaching it may be said that he is able to do so; but be that as it may: at Corinth the reality stood elsewhere!

For what diverse kinds of tongues had the Corinthians? Was it those freely given for edification by the one Spirit, or was it the clamour of contending parties, all speaking at once, and each determined to drown out the other?

Thus with the Corinthians it was indeed *divers kinds* – yes, and all at once – of *tongues*, note the plural. And though at the day of Pentecost by such wondrous heavenly gift the descended Holy Spirit marvellously glorified the ascended Christ, the promise of the Father filling as one the entire body, whilst they spake in the tongues of the nations of those about them, this was a far cry from – indeed, by Paul's gentle irony, it was *the very opposite to* – the clamour that existed at Corinth.

Hence, above even the best gifts, Paul yearned earnestly for his beloved children to discover the transcendent inner motive of 'a more excellent way': 'that ye all speak the same thing, and that there be no divisions among you; but that ye be perfectly joined together in the same mind and in the same judgment', I Corinthians 1:10.

Thus, by the nature of the true Gift; by the unity of the divine Giver; and by the appeal to the apostolic precedent, Paul almost imperceptibly guides them to the peerless divinity of the thirteenth chapter.

Ninth, and lastly, the apostle adds 'to another the interpretation of tongues'. Would God one among them, filled with the Spirit, and gifted by the grace of God, had interpreted for them *their* tongues, as they used them in practice, even as the gift of the Spirit, in peace and unity, interpreted the gift of another in the tongues sent down from heaven.

But now *their* tongues rose up on earth, and clashed in the flesh, and who shall interpret this?

Why, Paul shall, and that with a yearning love, a kindly wisdom, and the gentlest of implied rebukes, so that by the word of truth, by the power of God, and by the armour of righteousness, they might as one man be brought down in humility, conviction, self-condemnation, and heart-felt repentance.

And that is precisely what came to pass: 'For godly sorrow worketh repentance to salvation not to be repented of: but the sorrow of the world worketh death. For behold this selfsame thing, that ye sorrowed after a godly sort, what carefulness it wrought in you, yea, what clearing of yourselves, yea, what indignation, yea, what fear, yea, what vehement desire, yea, what zeal, yea, what revenge! In all things ye have approved yourselves to be clear in this matter', II Corinthians 7:10,11.

Then why did Paul stop at nine *charismata*, seeing that *ten* would have indicated completeness, in this case, of the *charismata*? Why? To draw attention to the fact that any number of gifts were as nothing without the Giver, that is, without God's unspeakable gift in the Son of his love, and, in truth, *that* was missing.

But as Paul continues from the twelfth chapter of the First Epistle to the Corinthians, he progresses from indicating their lack, to supplying their need by Christ Jesus in his doctrine unto them. Where? In the thirteenth chapter. Here he enlarges upon the missing, the tenth, the unspeakable gift of God.

Withal, thereby he sets forth unto them a more excellent way than all the gifts besides. How can this be? Because the chapter describes the indwelling of the Giver, one in deity with the Father and with the Son. 'Because the love of God is shed abroad in our hearts by the Holy Ghost which is given unto us', Romans 5:5.

Or as John put it, '*Herein* is our love made perfect'–or complete–I John 4:17.

However the *charismata*–the gifts of the Spirit in the body–objectively selected by way of admonitory instruction in I Corinthians 12:7-11, by no means embrace the entire compass of the various *charismata*, nor does that place represent the sole record of *charismata* in the new testament.

In Romans 12:6-8 Paul lists gifts–save for the one common instance of prophecy–whose range reaches to quite a different character, a range quite missing from I Corinthians 12:7-11, for all that the latter passage includes certain gifts omitted from the Romans text. Still the *range of character* is greater in Romans. Yet both–being gifts of the Spirit in the body–are called *charismata*.

Whereas Romans begins with prophecy, adding ministry, then teaching, and next exhortation–compatible in a sense with at least four, if not five, of the Corinthian *charismata*, since all are *vocal*–the last three *charisma* in Romans are distinct in essence from all those given in the Corinthian epistle. So much so, that one might be surprised that the three *were* gifts of the Spirit.

Observe: 'Giving'. Giving? What, at Corinth, where 'one is hungry, and another is drunken'; and, 'each one *taketh* before other *his own* supper'? See I Corinthians 11:21. Evidently, this singular gift in the body at Rome achieved in that assembly a far more gracious and benign effect from its presence and exercise.

Again, 'Ruling'. But who or what ruled at Corinth? Where, 'I speak to your shame. Is it so, that there is not a wise man among you? no, not one that shall be able to judge between his brethren?', I Corinthians 6:5. Rule? At Corinth? What rule, in that calamitous scene of chaos and disorder?

Then how beneficent and peaceable the gift of one for the blessing of all in rule by the Holy Ghost at Rome?

Lastly, 'Showing mercy'. But what mercy was shown to the brother in debt when taken to court by his creditor, I Corinthians 6:6,7? What mercy to the thirsty by the drunken, I Corinthians 11:21? What mercy to the hungry by the full, I Corinthians 11:21,22?

How Corinth would have benefited by the presence of this grace, this *charisma*, conspicuous at Rome, had it been present and in exercise among those who gloried in their contentious abuse of the nine gifts which, had even *they* been employed, might have spared the apostle the many tears and much anguish that forced him thus to write to his beloved children.

Whereas nine at Corinth indicates coming short of completeness, the seven at Rome points to the attainment of perfection. Then why are whole contemporary sects, and entire modern delusions, so enamoured of Corinth at its worst state – copying for all that they are worth, since the divine original and reality clean escape them – when the apostle labours with tears and anguish in his doctrine gently to deliver them?

I say, why so exalt the Corinthian *nine*, as if nothing perfect existed? Why? Because such ignorant persons are of the same carnal nature as that into which the Corinthians had fallen, but without their divine beginnings, and without the holy apostle to correct the lamentable issue.

Hence their inept misconstructions feed their lust for religious excitement, display, and even abandonment, the flesh – and the spirits – taking occasion through their blind perversion of the truth of the evangel of Christ, namely, of the apostles' doctrine, discipline, fellowship, and ordinances.

The apostle Peter likewise speaks of *charisma* – that is, gifts of the Spirit in the body of Christ – declaring 'As every man hath received the gift' – *charisma* – 'even so minister the same one toward another, as good stewards of the manifold grace of God.' This might well include Giving; Ruling; and Showing mercy, besides other gifts of like character.

However Peter goes on to emphasize that which is most to edification in their assembling together: 'If any man speak, let him speak as the oracles of God; if any man minister, let him do it as of the ability which God giveth: that God in all things may be glorified through Jesus Christ, to whom be praise and dominion for ever and ever. Amen', I Peter 4:10,11.

Where, note, as to being assembled together, the *charisma* to which Peter draws attention above all other relate, first, to 'speaking'. This must be 'as the oracles of God'. And this is only right, as befits the exercise of the gift of the Holy Ghost. Last, 'ministering', which as filled with the Spirit, and thus careful in the fear of God, must be of necessity 'as of the sufficiency which God giveth'.

Here we may well see the seven; yes, but where are the nine? Still going to the priest? Better the tenth, worshipping and pouring out thanksgiving at the feet of Jesus.

The tenth never got to the priest. Here is the *charisma* of mercy! Rather, the tenth saw where the healing truly lay, not only in this life, but in that which is to come. And he was a Samaritan; see Luke 17:11-19.

Before leaving this passage, I Corinthians 12:7-11, it is well to take notice of what are called 'miraculous' signs and gifts of the Spirit in the body of Christ: as though others, less conspicuous, were not. As has been said, *all* such gifts pertain *to the body of Christ*.

The *charismata* have nothing to do with the schisms, divisions, and denominations – not to mention independencies – into which Christendom has fallen. Nor have they to do with sects or movements *based on so-called manifestations*, which, in practice ignoring – as if it were of no consequence – I say, *ignoring* the unity of the body from which such schismatics are divided, namely *the body of Christ*, pretend to and mimic such things *as the end of their existence*.

What, schismatics mimic the manifestations which really did attend and glorified *the body of Christ* at the beginning? As if their invented human means at the last were more than the authenticated divine reality at the first? Or as if the apostles, the witness of Father, Son, and Holy Ghost, and the testimony of Holy Scripture might as well be ignored? Not to mention their blasphemous conjuring in order to beguile the foolish and the simple, as they ape that to which they have neither right, authority, justification, or calling.

However, it is remarkable that neither the apostle Peter, nor yet the apostle John, have *one word* to say of outwardly 'miraculous' *charisma*, much less of so-called 'tongues', witness I Peter 4:10,11, where the entire emphasis is on gifts of the Spirit in speaking and ministering. As to John, he does not so much as mention *charismata*, or, indeed, *any* miraculous signs in the *ecclesia*, though he has three epistles, one revelation, and seven churches in which to do so.

Besides this, Paul says *nothing of that kind of sign or manifestation* in Romans 12:6-8, a passage just as much devoted to *charismata* as is I Corinthians 12:7-11.

Regarding the later epistles, or the ministers of God under and following the apostles, besides the all-important pastoral epistles – *indicating what should follow after the apostles' departure* – the silence is deafening. Not because the Holy Ghost did not indwell the *ecclesia* just as much as at the beginning, or that the gifts of the Spirit were given to *any less a number than every man in the assembly;* but because the emphasis – as indicated by Romans, Peter, and the Johannine epistles – *lay upon those vocal gifts by which the apostles' doctrine should be reiterated spiritually to the end of the age.*

Not that these vocal gifts were *less* miraculous, or *less* of the Spirit: but, so much the more as the end approached, *they were the more necessary.*

Besides, the miraculous signs and wonders wrought by the apostles, and through the laying on of their hands, and in the manifestation of the gifts of that one and the selfsame Spirit in the one body, *had more than sufficiently given testimony by miracles, signs and wonders* to the witness of God that this was *his ecclesia.* Just as had the wonders wrought in the land of Ham, and the signs shown in the field of Zoan, when Israel came out of Egypt.

And what shall I more say of the parting of the Red Sea, the bringing of water out of the rock, the descent of the heavenly manna, or the terrible judgments by which Jehovah bore record to his authority resting upon Moses and Aaron?

These are to be remembered continually, as the psalmist often exhorts us. But, given, did these things cross over Jordan with them? Did the Rock follow them after they came into the land? Did the manna still fall when they ate the finest of the wheat in their inheritance? Did the Red Sea continue parting at the words of 'faith' by zealots long afterwards? Certainly not.

The previous signs, miracles, wonders and manifestations were more than sufficient to give divine attestation to Israel's beginnings, but they merely *attended* the giving of the law, and of the testimony, and of the prophetic word. Having been given, repetition—divorced from their original significance—would have *distracted* from what was *actually* central and *really* abiding.

Had these signs continued—human nature being what it is—such passing wonders would have appeared to man as vastly more significant and important than the vital, permanent, and everlasting *truth*. That is, *unalterable* and *absolute* truth, in the giving of which miracles were no more than transient and suitably placed signposts for future generations to mark and read in the unfolding passage of time.

Witness the worship of the brazen serpent, which had long since ceased to have any significance. Yet, because *once* it was vested with miraculous powers, thereafter the superstitious and credulous bowed down and craved present signs and wonders on the basis of its past history. However, the righteous ground it to powder.

Therefore miracles, once having been given, passed away. But, 'To the law and to the testimony, if they speak not *according to this word*, it is because there is no light in them.'

Then, let the people rejoice in the remembrances of their beginnings; but *now*, let them attend upon the testimony of Israel, the law of Moses, the judgments given to Jacob, the prophetic word, and, indeed, to that which was committed to them, namely, the oracles of God.

Just so in the *ecclesia*. We need every part as much of the divine indwelling as they had in the beginning; we need every whit as much of the appropriate gifts of the Spirit in the assembly as were theirs at the first; but, whilst remembering with joy the original apostolic witness, we know that our need is for that which is appropriate for us *today*, that we may *keep alive in the new testament, that is, in the testimony of Jesus, which is the Spirit of prophecy.*

I say, we need these divine and inward things to remember and declare the words of our Lord Jesus Christ and his holy apostles; to keep the faith; to obey from the heart the form of doctrine delivered unto us; to hear continually the apostles' doctrine reiterated by the Holy Ghost; to have the doctrine of Christ sound in our ears constantly.

We need these things to hear the Lord's voice in the assembly; yes, and to witness the distribution of the suited gifts—even according to the closing record of the new testament scriptures—by that one and the selfsame Spirit, that, holding fast the form of sound words, we might abide in that which was—and is—central from the beginning.

And what was—and is—central from the beginning? The apostles' doctrine and fellowship, the breaking of bread and prayers, for in the hearing and continuance of this lies our salvation and safety, even as it is said, 'truly our fellowship is with the Father, and with his Son Jesus Christ'.

In a word, we need to continue—to abide—in one Spirit, abundantly able to give gifts to every man in the unity of this one body, suited to the times and conditions of the recovery of these selfsame things in our own age.

III

The Spirit and the Body

'FOR as the body is one, and hath many members, and all the members of that one body, being many, are one body: so also is the Christ', I Corinthians 12:12.

Observe the words 'For as', indicating that what follows is either an explanation, illustration, or analogy of what had been said before.

What had been said before? 'All these'–manifestations of the Spirit between one and another among many brethren – 'all these worketh that one and the selfsame Spirit'– that is, they are a variety of supernatural yet audible and visible manifestations *which show that one divine person spiritually and invisibly indwells the entire number of the assembled saints in unity.*

However, that one divine, invisible and spiritual person manifests his presence in unity 'dividing to every man severally as he will', I Corinthians 12:11.

23

Now Paul is to illustrate and open this spiritual mystery–albeit this divine reality–by an analogy: it is the analogy of the body. To introduce this, he uses the words 'For as'.

'For as the body is one, and hath many members, and all the members of that one body, being many, are one body.' Here he shows the relation of the members to the body.

Not only has the body many members, but each one of that number is essential to make up the whole. The whole is called the body, and this whole is much, much more than the sum of the parts.

Nevertheless *each single part*–or every member–is necessary if one is to speak of the body as a whole. The absence of but one–though it be the very least–member precludes having a sound body. All together *are* the body. Their union *constitutes* the body.

Considered in themselves, each is a member. Together, they are many members. In union they are the body.

The explanation, the visible illustration, the analogy is clearly apparent. Let this, however, be pressed home: the body as a whole is comprised of many members in particular, yet so united as to present a visible, tangible organic entity.

Physically the members grow into and are connected together as one. The bones support all; the sinews connect all; the joints give movement to all; the flesh covers all; the breathing aerates all; the blood replenishes all; the nerves sensitize all; the circulation renews all; the skin encloses all: yes, but above all, *the life quickens all*. Now, here is much more than the sum of many members. *The body is more than all.*

Now, declares Paul, 'So also is the Christ', I Corinthians 12:12. Properly translated–as opposed to transliterated and truncated–

this should read 'So also is *the Anointed*'. Incidentally, note the definite article.

But the anointing is not that of oil poured out by Moses upon the head of Aaron the high priest, flowing down to the skirts of his garments, and therefore covering all members – which was a tangible figure – it is of the *Holy Ghost*, which is an intangible reality.

Then, it is not outward, but inward. It is not visible, but invisible. It is not human, but divine. It is not earthly, it is heavenly. It is not natural, it is supernatural.

Maybe: *but it still flows down from the Head and it still covers – or, rather, fills – all the members in one body, one with and united to the Head.*

Then the members, which, with the Head, constitute that one body, are seen as one with him, and hence it is said in consequence of the anointing, 'So also is the Anointed', or, 'So also is the Christ'.

That is, so also is *his* body. It is one, tempered together in union; it has many members, united together in one, each member having his own place in the body. There are many members, yes, but all are necessary to make up the whole.

The united whole constitutes his body; less does not: the whole is in obvious and undeniable union, each essential member in his place, and all united together as an entity. This is true of the entire *ecclesia*, and it is represented in the manifold wisdom of God in *each ecclesia*.

Manifested: though spiritual and invisible in the *anointing*, it is visible and manifest in the unity.

For Paul is speaking of *the assembly*. This is evident through the unity of the brethren. Are *they* invisible? As it pertains to their union with Christ, and with the Holy Ghost, and in their interior *spiritual* union with each other, yes.

But since *that interior union* separates them from the world to be together as one, and since that separation is *to the assembly, visible in their assembling, then, visible indeed.*

For, whatever is inward, it is *within their bodies*. And *in the body* they are assembled. Then, their unity is abundantly—*and bodily*—made manifest. 'So also is the Christ.'

It is true, in the anointing, of each member it is said, 'he that is joined to the Lord is one spirit'. Yes, but the '*he*' that is so joined in one spirit, is, in and of himself, in the body. As it is written, 'Know ye not that *your bodies* are the members of Christ?'—or, of the Anointed?—I Corinthians 6:15,17.

Then—*bodily*—it must follow, however divine, however supernatural, however mystical, however spiritual, however invisible *this inward union*, it is of *absolute necessity that it becomes corporeally visible in the* gathering of the *assembly*: 'So also is the Christ.'

It is worthy of note that 'there are diversities of gifts, but the same Spirit', I Corinthians 12:4, corresponds with verses 7-11, namely, *what the Spirit is to the body, and the body to the Spirit.* Just as 'There are differences of ministries, but the same Lord', I Corinthians 12:5, answers to verses 12-27, that is, *what the Lord is to the body, and the body to the Lord.*

One thing is certain: there is nothing individual in itself, much less independent, in either case: *everything* is corporate, whether in the whole *ecclesia*, or in any given manifestation of that whole, for example, at Corinth.

This observation utterly cuts out all denominationalism, every form of independency, and each affectation of individualism, including sects based on the *notion* of one body, whilst in doctrine and practice denying it, such as the various schisms of Brethrenism, besides those founded on an entirely false interpretation of the baptism of the Spirit, such as Pentecostalism in its many divisions, including the craze of the 'Charismatic' delusion.

On the contrary, as to both the gifts of the Spirit and the administrations from the Lord, *there is one body, to which corresponds one Spirit*: 'One body, and one Spirit, even as ye are called in one hope of your calling; One Lord, one faith, one baptism, one God and Father of all, who is above all, and through all, and in you all', Ephesians 4:4-6. 'So also is the Christ', I Corinthians 12:12.

The members of his body are so inwardly joined, ingrafted, grown together, and interconnected as one in the Spirit–'their hearts being *knit together* in love'–that the outward manifestation of this interior unity is clear and plain to all.

They themselves visibly present–in each place, and all in every place–I say, they themselves present a real, visible and manifest unity, a united company, a separated assembly, a mystery of union and communion in one and the selfsame Spirit, that nothing else will suffice as an analogy but to say, They are 'one body'. That is, So also is the Christ.

But not as it were the literal body of a person, who in and of himself fills that body with his own life. For the apostle speaks in a mystery of *the body of Christ*.

It is *his* life that fills the one body, both as a whole, and as manifest in each place. It is *God's* power that sustains that one body, *his* energy, in every place, and in all places joined as one. It is the *Spirit's* anointing that bestows the interior fulness, in each several manifestation of the one body, and in that one body in itself as a whole. 'So also is the Christ.'

So that it is not simply a question of persons in spiritual agreement, or sharing a common spiritual experience. It is *the indwelling of divine persons.*

In particular, I Corinthians 12, the indwelling of the person of the Holy Ghost; for this is in the context of 'spiritualities'. In this passage the body is not mentioned in connection with the Head in heaven, much less is it, itself, seen as in the heavenlies.

In First Corinthians *the body is seen on earth, as constituted by the divine person of the Holy Ghost, descended so as to indwell the whole in his own person.* This is that one and the selfsame Spirit the manifestation of whose gifts, both supernatural and diverse, declare in their unity the invisible but unmistakable presence of the divine Giver, the one indwelling person of the Holy Spirit of God: 'So also is the Christ.'

The Authorized Version renders the first part of the next verse, 'For by one Spirit are we all baptized into one body', I Corinthians 12:13, but this translation is not correct. It could not be correct, not only because it misrepresents the Greek, but also because it contradicts what is asserted elsewhere.

What is asserted elsewhere? Why, that *Christ* baptizes with the Holy Ghost. Matthew 3:11, '*he* shall baptize you with the Holy Ghost'; Mark 1:8, '*he* shall baptize you with the Holy Ghost'; Luke 3:16, '*he* shall baptize you with the Holy Ghost'.

Is not this testimony enough to establish the truth that the one who baptizes with the Holy Ghost is Jesus Christ, the Son of God?

If not, hear once more from the record of John the Baptist: 'And John bare record, saying, I saw the Spirit descending from heaven like a dove, and it abode upon him. And I knew him not: but he that sent me to baptize with water, the same said unto me, Upon whom thou shalt see the Spirit descending, and remaining on him, *the same is he which baptizeth with the Holy Ghost. And I saw, and bare record that this is the Son of God*, John 1:32-34.

Whence it is evident – from all four gospels – beyond all controversy that it is the Lord Jesus Christ, the Son of God, and he alone, who baptizes with the Holy Ghost.

Then why have the Authorized Version translators contradicted this – and thus confounded the English reader – by declaring: 'For *by one Spirit* are we all baptized into one body', I Corinthians 12:13, where, they say, *the Spirit himself* baptizes, namely, baptizes all into one body?

Then, according to them, since it is clear that the baptism referred to is that of the Holy Ghost, the Spirit himself both does the baptizing and is the baptism.

For if by the Spirit we are baptized, then, *the Spirit baptizes of his own Spirit*. If so, not content with contradicting the clear fourfold testimony of the gospels, the translators go on to make the verse a confusion – if not a nonsense – within itself.

Then what ought it to read, and where lies the error? This place *ought* to read, 'For *in* one Spirit are we all baptized into one body'; that is, the *Son of God* baptizes all into one body *in one Spirit*.

The error lies in mistranslating the Greek preposition ἐv, *en*. The translators at once contradicted all four gospels, confounded divine persons, obscured the work of God, and made a nonsense of the verse, by imposing the English word 'by', as if it translated the Greek '*en*'.

It does not. It confuses it. The Greek is translated properly by the preposition 'in', giving the correct sense, 'For in one Spirit are we all baptized into one body', I Corinthians 12:13.

The translators have no excuse whatsoever. They had good precedents in any case, but *would* follow the wrong ones. Rightly, Tyndale, 1535, rendered '*en*' as 'in'. And so did Coverdale, 1535.

Thereafter – with almost unbroken monotony – the succession of translators – all we like sheep have gone astray: that is, one after the other, seeing nothing but the backside of the sheep in front – mangle the Greek, make this place to confound itself, contradict the gospels, and, in truth, make a mock of divinity.

The Great Bible, 1540, begins this confusion, despite the correct translations of its predecessors. No, they must change 'in' for 'by', as if the Greek were irrelevant beside their confounded prevarications.

This error was followed by the Geneva Bible, 1562, and the Bishops Bible, 1602. The Roman Catholic Rheims Version, 1582, shames these Protestants, upholding against them the correct translation 'in'.

Not so the next Protestant Bible, namely the King James – or Authorized Version – of 1611, which follows the corruption 'by'.

To the contrary, notwithstanding the committee having been duped by Westcott and Hort, the Revised Version, 1881, with its sly substitution of a Greek edition based on sheer fallacy, yet gives the correct 'in'. Alas! must we be shamed by these also?

The Revised Standard Version, 'updating' the Revision of 1881 in 1946, boldly peels off the sheep's clothing of superficial corrections and reverts to type, much more comfortable in the wolf-skin of 'by'.

So there you have your clerical and 'scholarly' record.

Young – of Concordance fame – emphatically insists upon 'in': 'For also in one Spirit we all to one body were baptized.'

I suppose I should quote J.N. Darby, who renders this part of the verse with characteristic and imperious assumption: 'For also in [the power of] one Spirit we have all been baptized into one body', where the words in brackets actually are pure invention, like so many of those Brethren traditions and conceits that still manage to persuade the ignorant that their outward forms, unwarranted assumptions, and impertinent conclusions are 'scriptural', or, as they now like to put it – irrespective of version – 'bible based'. But enough of this miserable dust.

The text reads in fact 'For also in one Spirit are we all baptized into one body.'

Also? 'For also'? As well as what? To get the sense, read the context: 'So also is the Christ.' Or, rather, 'the Anointed'. Hence in continuity the passage is as follows: 'So also is the Anointed. For also in one Spirit are we all baptized into one body.'

Where the anointing, under the Anointed, inwardly flowing down upon and into every member, is likened – also – to the baptism of the Spirit, just as the baptism of the Spirit – 'for also' – is much like to the anointing.

Where is the difference?

The anointing pertains to that divine, interior, mysterious, and spiritual unction in which God marks us out by the Holy Ghost as being united to Christ: it is the infallible mark that we are his, and one with him under the anointing.

The baptism of the Spirit is in a sense more intimate. It brings in *one body*. It is not only that the members are anointed, marked out as Christ's by the Spirit, but by the baptism of the Spirit, the Spirit himself *indwells all the members in his own person, so as to constitute the whole one body in Christ*: 'So also is the Anointed. For also in one Spirit are we all baptized into one body', I Corinthians 12:12,13.

31

The expression 'Baptism of the Holy Ghost' occurs some seven times in the new testament.

The words were first spoken by John the Baptist before the baptism of Jesus, and are recorded respectively in Matthew, Mark, and Luke, each referring to the same occasion.

The fourth reference is in John, who records the Baptist's testimony to the Son of God—that it is he who shall baptize with the Holy Ghost—shortly after the baptism of Jesus.

Observe that in the first three gospels the Baptist prophesies, 'He shall baptize *you* with the Holy Ghost', where *you* refers to those penitent Jews who had received and obeyed the prophetic ministry of John, having confessed their sins and been baptized of him in Jordan.

Without doubt some, and in all probability all, of the number of the apostles had received the baptism of John. Exceptions are possible, but unlikely.

In the unlikely event, then they would have been baptized by the first disciples, 'Jesus made and baptized more disciples than John, though Jesus himself baptized not, but his disciples', John 4:1,2.

As to all the apostles being baptized—probably by John, but otherwise by the first disciples—observe, 'Except a man be born of *water* and of the Spirit, he cannot enter into the kingdom of God', John 3:5.

And how could the apostles, who were sent of Christ to preach the kingdom of God, not first themselves have entered into it? And, if so, initially by water.

In the evangel according to John, the prophecy that the Son would baptize with the Holy Ghost is not confined to the 'you', namely, to the repentant and obedient remnant out of all Israel.

John broadens the scope, declaring of the Son of God, 'The same is he which baptizeth with the Holy Ghost', John 1:33, where the whole emphasis is upon the one who baptizes, not those who are baptized.

Thus John hints of a people far beyond the remnant according to the election of grace called out from among the Jews. 'Is he the God of the Jews only? is he not also of the Gentiles? Yes, of the Gentiles also', Romans 3:29.

After the first four references to the baptism of the Holy Ghost—Matthew, Mark, Luke, and John respectively—two further instances appear in the Acts of the Apostles.

Jesus, risen from the dead and appearing to the apostles whom he had chosen, virtually repeats the words which the Baptist spoke in Matthew, Mark, and Luke: 'For John truly baptized with water; but ye shall be baptized with the Holy Ghost not many days hence', Acts 1:5.

Likewise in Acts 11:16, Peter, giving an account of the way in which the Holy Ghost fell upon the devout Gentiles, reiterates words previously spoken: 'And as I began to speak, the Holy Ghost fell on them, as on us at the beginning. Then remembered I the word of the Lord, how that he said, John indeed baptized with water; but ye shall be baptized with the Holy Ghost. Forasmuch then as God gave them the like gift as he did unto us, who believed on the Lord Jesus Christ; what was I, that I could withstand God?', Acts 11:15-17.

This quotation—Acts 11:15-17—is the sixth occasion on which the expression Baptism of—or in this case, be baptized with—the Holy Ghost appears in the new testament, and the second in Acts. The seventh and last incidence is in I Corinthians 12:13, the text in question.

However the exposition of this place is not just a matter of the seven occasions on which the actual expression 'Baptism of the Holy Ghost' occurs: indeed, the *words* are not used in Acts 2, the very chapter describing the descent and shedding forth of the person of the Holy Ghost to fill the one hundred and twenty disciples in the upper room, when they were all together with one accord in one place on the day of Pentecost.

Moreover there are two further instances in which what occurred answers so nearly to Acts chapter 2 that—though, like Acts 2, not actually called the baptism of the Spirit in the text—these occasions undoubtedly refer to a repetition of the same thing.

The first concerns the Samaritans, Acts 8:16,17, the second the—presumably—Gentile disciples at Ephesus, Acts 19:2-6.

In both cases note the laying on of the hands of those called to the apostolate: 'Then they'—namely Peter and John—'laid their hands on them'—that is, the Samaritans who had believed Philip's preaching and had been baptized in the name of the Lord Jesus, yet upon whom the Holy Ghost had 'not yet fallen'; but when the apostles laid their hands on them—*then* 'they received the Holy Ghost'.

In the other case the disciples at Ephesus, who knew no more than and had received nothing save John's baptism, thereafter, when Christ Jesus was preached unto them, were—again—baptized, this time in the name of the Lord Jesus. 'And when Paul had laid his hands upon them, the Holy Ghost came on them; and they spake with tongues, and prophesied. And all the men were about twelve', Acts 19:2-7.

Furthermore, there are passages in at least two of the epistles which indicate that those concerned had been baptized with the Holy Ghost on a previous occasion, namely, when first they had received the grace of God.

'Truly the signs of an apostle were wrought among you in all patience, in signs, and wonders, and mighty deeds', II Corinthians

12:12, although nothing of this is mentioned in the narrative of the beginning of the work of the Lord at Corinth, Acts chapter 18.

Again, 'He therefore that ministereth to you the Spirit, and worketh miracles among you, doeth he it by the works of the law, or by the hearing of faith?', Galatians 3:5. But there is no record of this in Acts or anywhere else.

Quite apart from these specific instances, there are suggestions from the early ministry of the apostles—particularly in the case of Paul—that not only the baptism of the Holy Ghost, but miracles, signs, and wonders followed of necessity, given to those called into the *ecclesia* by the evangel of Christ.

I say, 'into the *ecclesia*', for, observe, it is 'He shall baptize *you*'—not *thee*—'with the Holy Ghost', Matthew 3:11; Mark 1:8; and Luke 3:16. Likewise, 'For also in one Spirit *are all we* baptized into *one body*', I Corinthians 12:13.

Then, the baptism brings in *that which is corporate*. It is not at all individual, save that the individual is incorporated into the one body of Christ.

Whence it follows that the end in view with the baptism of the Spirit is not so much what *he* is for *me*. It is altogether what *we* are for *him*, united together as one body in Christ.

IV

The Baptism of the Spirit

OF tongues I shall have occasion to speak later, but it is *essential* to note that tongues *no more than accompanied* the baptism of the Holy Ghost on certain notable occasions. If so, they were, as such, distinct from that baptism, in and of itself.

Then, the baptism of the Holy Ghost could and did—according to the narrative—occur without the speaking in tongues, for example, as in the case of the Samaritans, Acts 8:15-18.

No mention of tongues appears in Romans, Thessalonians, Philippians or Galatians, for example: but it is unquestionable that all these were baptized with the Holy Ghost.

On the other hand, silence does not necessarily imply absence: note that the first Ephesian disciples—when Paul the apostle laid hands on them—received the Holy Ghost 'and'—immediately—'spake with tongues, and prophesied', Acts 19:6. Yet in the great epistle to the saints at Ephesus, Paul, writing much later, makes no mention of tongues.

So that even from the earliest days of the apostles it is necessary to observe that the incomparable gift of the baptism of the Holy Ghost, so as to form one body in Christ, vastly transcended – and transcends – the sign of tongues which by no means necessarily accompanied that baptism.

Moreover, whilst the laying on of the apostles' hands – subsequent to Acts 2 – appeared in a number of cases as that which conveyed the baptism of the Holy Ghost, this was not invariably the case. Note the instance of Cornelius: 'While Peter was yet *speaking*' – not while Peter was yet *laying on hands*, of which nothing whatsoever is said – 'the Holy Ghost fell on all them which heard the word', Acts 10:44.

So that hasty and rash conclusions should be avoided. At this point what one may safely deduce is that the baptism of the Holy Ghost is a thing in and of itself; it is not at all a thing which must necessarily be followed by the sign of tongues; again, that the baptism of the Holy Ghost invariably followed and was never disassociated from the effectual preaching of the apostles' doctrine, and at that, in the new testament, by the very apostles themselves.

Moreover the laying on of the apostles' hands was not necessarily a criterion. The preaching was a criterion, under which the hearing of faith became manifest by the baptism of the Holy Ghost.

Finally, one should mention that the significant manifestations in Acts answer to the words of the Lord Jesus immediately preceding the ascension: 'Ye' – that is, *the apostles whom he had chosen*, Acts 1:2 – 'Ye shall be witnesses unto me both in Jerusalem, and in all Judea, and in Samaria, and unto the uttermost part of the earth', Acts 1:8.

Jerusalem, Judea, and Samaria are obvious, from Acts chapter 2 to Acts chapter 8.

'The uttermost part of the earth'–within the limits of Acts–has a twofold testimony in the significant baptism of the Gentiles, first of Cornelius' gathering, Acts 10, then that of those at Ephesus, Acts 19.

What remains is that one should remember that–taking for granted the addition of I Corinthians 12:13–*these references include, and, with objective fairness, expand, the–only–seven occurrences of the expression, the baptism of the Holy Ghost*. Then, a sense of proportion must be maintained, especially in relation to the many–and *later*–works and books recorded in the remainder of the new testament.

For example, whilst unquestionably the baptism of the Holy Ghost–*let it always be remembered, given so as to constitute the body of Christ, exclusively and invariably*–must have occurred in the later epistles; yet neither that, nor any miraculous signs–unless it were the deceitful duplications of the Adversary–appear in the closing records.

Nothing could be more conspicuous by dint of absence than either the words 'baptism of the Spirit', or any *charismata* whatsoever, in the Pastoral Epistles. Yet these were written to ensure the continuation of the apostolic ministry and fellowship in the apostle's absence. Hence these scriptures were of paramount importance for those approaching the end of the apostolic presence and close of the new testament. And if so, how much more for us from that time to this? So why the silence concerning the baptism and the miraculous gifts?

Take the other later epistles. Peter was a chosen eyewitness. He was at Pentecost. No one had more experience. He gave forth the first words after the baptism and shedding forth of the Holy Ghost at the very first. Likewise he explained the reason for and nature of the tongues with which they then spake: then *why no mention of any of these things in the very much later First and Second Epistles of Peter?*

The baptism, evidently, was taken for granted as having taken place. As to miracles, these, apparently, as with Israel of old, had fulfilled their office: *the thing signified, the reality itself, remained.* And this Peter addressed.

Nothing in Jude, I, II, and III John? But John, like Peter, had been at the heart of the matter in Acts 2. But no word of this in the three later–if not last–epistles.

Why not? Only one explanation adequately answers this question. Miracles had fulfilled their office. That to which they *had* borne testimony under the apostles and apostolic churches remained on record in Acts and the earlier Epistles–or, indeed, the Gospels–just as the testimony of the Pentateuch–particularly Exodus and Numbers–remain on record for Israel in the succeeding millennia till the coming of Christ.

Then what corresponding apostolic testimony? This. *This* is the *heart* of that testimony: 'the word of the Lord endureth for ever. And *this* is the *word* which by the *gospel* is *preached* unto you', I Peter 1:25. The eternal Spirit bore –and bears–equal witness to that word of the truth of the gospel, and will bear it, in all those sent of Jesus Christ to the end of the age, for the Spirit is truth.

The Book of Revelation? Seven churches, yes, but neither a single mention nor one hint of the baptism of the Spirit, or of miraculous gifts. But signs, wonders, miracles, and delusions– for the last times–in abundance from Satan and the second beast. 'To the law and to the testimony: if they speak not according to this word, it is because they have no light in them', Isaiah 8:20.

In conclusion, consider the last word on this very matter, recorded in yet another of the later epistles, one written under no less an authority than the Apostle of our profession.

'How shall we escape, if we neglect so great salvation'–not, neglect so great a *baptism*; nor so great *signs*: but, not neglect the *reality*; not neglect *the thing signified*, namely, *so great salvation*– 'which at the first began to be spoken'–mark that, *what matters is conveyed by speech*–'spoken by the Lord, and was confirmed unto us'–where *us* is a further generation, like ourselves–'unto us by them that heard him'–that is, confirmed unto us by the apostles that heard him, in the first generation–'God *also* bearing *them* witness'–that is *also* meaning *as well as* bearing witness to the Lord when *he* spoke: *also* bearing witness to the chosen apostles and eyewitnesses, when, in turn, *they* spoke–'God also bearing *them* witness'–not *us* witness: *them* witness–'both with signs and wonders, and with divers miracles, and gifts of the Holy Ghost, according to his own will?', Hebrews 2:4.

Just as the manna ceased, the pillar of cloud and fire departed, the water from the Rock which followed them withdrew, having fulfilled their office when Israel entered into the land, so it is with us, in terms of the apostolic signs, since we have entered by so great salvation into the rest that remains for the people of God, being baptized into one body in one Spirit, our signs– the signs of the *new* covenant–likewise having reached the satisfactory conclusion of their abundant witness.

What remains? These things remain: 'There is one body, and one Spirit, even as ye are called in one hope of your calling; One Lord, one faith, one baptism; One God and Father of all, who is above all, and through all, and in you all', Ephesians 4:4-6.

The gospel–the evangel–abides; the baptism of the Spirit remains. The fellowship of the apostles, which is with the Father, and with his Son Jesus Christ, that continues.

But I repeat, the *signs* of an apostle, the generation of the apostles, these have ceased, having fulfilled their purpose. But the word of the Lord endureth for ever. The Son is upon his Father's throne, the Spirit abides below: *these bear witness to the evangel, the doctrine of Christ*. The vain pursuit of signs and wonders–once having been given under the safe hands of the apostles–but diverts attention from the one thing needful in the things that abide.

The facts speak for themselves. Nothing less than what has been said *explains the facts*, both then at the first, thereafter till the close of Revelation, and since, even until this present time.

I am obliged to add that not only – over a lifetime – am I aware of 'Pentecostal' and 'Charismatic' claims concerning miracles, signs, wonders, healings, and of course 'tongues', in modern times, but that I have without prejudice in my early days – before being established more perfectly by the Spirit of truth in vital experience by Holy Scripture – having first been converted at twenty years old, entered enthusiastically into their extravagances. But out of them all the Lord delivered me.

Moreover, since then, far from sitting in an armchair or at some comfortable meeting and gullibly swallowing up everything dished out by 'Pentecostal' and like-minded 'missionaries' in the 'Foreign field' to the 'Home base' – namely, from primitive countries to America and Britain – I have gone to see for myself.

In every case of close enquiry and examination of those whom the scriptures call the heathen, I found exaggeration, more than equalled by the superstitious witchcraft to which such excitable, ignorant and credulous poor people were already prone. Some instances could not be explained naturally, but that was very rare, and in any event matched by spiritual evil and followed by blasphemy.

Likewise I found neither the reality of the doctrine of Christ, nor the *true* inward work of the Holy Ghost – read 'Saving Faith' – nor yet the love of *the truth*. There was no question of the superabounding enthusiasm, sacrifice, or sincerity of the peoples so easily swayed.

But let armchair and excitable – nevertheless sedentary – meeting enthusiasts remember that the financial support of these 'missionaries' – together with those of the Society backing them – increases in proportion to the tales of miraculous wonders reported from 'the field' to the 'home base'.

Let them also remember that a fool and his money are soon parted. I may add, so also are self-styled 'Pentecostals' and 'Charismatics' parted, not merely from sound common sense, but – not at all infrequently – quite literally from all reason.

And let not these – or anyone else – accuse me of limiting the power of God. They invent it; we proclaim it: but as it is in truth, that is, in the full inworking of so great salvation, together with the revelation both of the person and work of the Holy Ghost in glorifying Christ by the evangel.

I say, We proclaim it: and we do so as called of God, declaring nothing but that which agrees and harmonizes with that tenor of doctrine, narrative and fellowship commanded by the Lord to be followed faithfully after the decease of the apostles.

More: unlike these erroneous persons, I teach according to the doctrine of Christ and his holy apostles the *truth* of the baptism of the Holy Ghost, namely, that it is always to bring in and to incorporate into *one body*, about which I have found these fanatics totally ignorant, though it pertains to the most precious things of the inner sanctuary. But then, What do they care about *the love of the truth, that they might be saved?*

Rather, their trust is in so-called manifestations, supposed signs, and in what they presume to be the Spirit, yet a spirit who speaks of himself, glorifies them, and has little or no interest in *the truth.*

Is that plain enough English for you?

Of course there is a baptism of the Holy Ghost: I have expounded it to you as it is in holy writ. But *one body in Christ always follows from it.* Of course the Spirit gives gifts – 'charismata' – but neither in the perfect list of these in Romans, nor in Peter – and who knows best, he or them? – do they appear as *outwardly* miraculous.

And of course the baptism even today is given to those who seek one body in Christ. But not to those who ignore it, who glorify themselves by pretending to it, who rend the body of Christ by forming a sect over it, and who say and do not.

That is, they say over and over 'baptism of the Spirit', yet in works do not have it, but rather deny it in its very essence and divine purpose by their unruly pretence.

However, as to those who know and love the truth, though they have erred and gone out of the way, nevertheless by grace it abides true of them, 'For also in one Spirit are we all baptized into one body', I Corinthians 12:13.

The origin of the words 'baptize with the Holy Ghost' is to be found in the ministry of John the Baptist, in a prophecy concerning Christ which contrasts *Christ's coming ministry with John's present one*. 'I indeed baptize you with water, but he shall baptize you with the Holy Ghost', Matthew 3:11, Mark 1:8, and Luke 3:16.

Nevertheless, contrast or not, John's baptism not only prefigured that of Christ, it was a visible earthly manifestation of that invisible heavenly effusion which was to come.

Therefore the baptism of John was a *figure* of the baptism of the Holy Ghost, and, in fact, the latter expression is derived from the former, so that John prophesied of Christ baptizing from the ascended glory–having received the promise of the Holy Ghost from the Father in view of the completion and perfection of his substitutionary work on earth–I say, John prophesied of this in terms of his own faithful work in baptizing the penitent Jews in the river Jordan.

John baptized in the wilderness, and preached the baptism of repentance for the remission of sins to the Jews–and to all that remained of the remnant of Israel–saying, 'Repent ye: for the kingdom of heaven is at hand', adding, 'I indeed baptize you with water unto repentance: but he that cometh after me is mightier than I, whose shoes I am not worthy to bear: he shall baptize you with the Holy Ghost, and with fire.'

This mighty word was with power, for the Holy Ghost was upon John, and from the beginning of his preaching in the wilderness 'there went out to him Jerusalem, and all Judea, and all the region round about Jordan, and were baptized of him in Jordan, confessing their sins.'

Here was the repentant remnant of the election according to grace. These repented with a repentance not to be repented of, filled with contrition and godly sorrow, openly confessing their sins, and publicly being baptized of John.

What was the vision before them? The One that should come after John, who was mightier than he, who should baptize them with the Holy Ghost, bringing in the Kingdom of God, which was at hand.

For they knew, they sensed, it was witnessed in their hearts, 'Except a man be born of water and of the Spirit, he cannot enter into the kingdom of God', John 3:5.

Hence they were baptized unto John's baptism, thus to be born of water, looking and searching earnestly for the One of whom John spake, because he would baptize them with the Holy Ghost, that they might be born of the Spirit, and enter into the Kingdom of God.

Neither shall this fail of application, nor shall the spiritual voice of John crying in the inward wilderness of the soul cease, preparing the way of the Lord, till the Lord comes again.

These things are spiritual, but of them Paul would not have you to be ignorant, but discerning, for it remains a truth that whoso climbs up some other way is a thief and a robber.

Now consider the significance of John's baptism as–in a figure– it opens the mystery of the Son of God baptizing with one Spirit into one body, where those thus baptized are viewed as the members of his body.

This cannot be envisaged naturally, for the simple reason that the members of one's body are not only a corporeal whole, they are energized by the same vitality; quickened by the same life; they are sensitized by the same nervous system; renewed by the same life-giving blood; replenished by the same breathing; upheld by the same skeletal system; are of one physical appearance; have the same joints and bands; are clothed with the same supple skin; are of distinct physical integration; are of singular visible composition; and, above all, are the possession of that unique living soul whose outward structure is thus constituted as a physical entity–in itself unique–in the oneness of its many members.

Together these many members make up the material composition of the unity of one person's body: But how can *many* such persons–each with his own separate bodily frame–no matter how united in mind and heart, be regarded as the *members* of the *one* body of Christ? How can this be explained?

Mysteries cannot be explained. But by spiritual experience they can be both opened and unveiled. And they can be signified in a figure.

Therefore, again, consider John's baptism. Here were the bodies of many persons, who, having received in their hearts and minds the searching words of John the Baptist, confessed their sins, and alike waded into the river Jordan to be baptized of John.

One river; but many immersions. One river; but poured out over many. Many immersions, but into one Jordan; many on whom the waters were poured out, but waters from one and the same river.

Thus, when John baptized, all the many penitents stood in the water, and out of the water.

More or less of every one of their bodies was submerged, so that what appeared seemed—as it were beneath the surface—to be invisibly united the one to the other by the same river in which all stood and out of which that which was visible of each one emerged. So it was when John baptized. His disciples stood in and were united by that depth of the one flowing river.

Moreover, that of their bodies which did appear above the surface of the water shone all wet and glistening with the waters of baptism poured out over them. But the waters were one, and were from one and the same river.

Then said John, 'I indeed baptize you with water'—*thus* he baptized them with water—'but he shall baptize you with the Holy Ghost.'

Now, the Spirit is likened to the river of the water of life or to the water from the smitten Rock which followed Israel in the wilderness. Which Rock, saith Paul, was Christ. But the water from that Rock signified the Holy Ghost, which Christ—once smitten—having been exalted, received of the Father, and shed forth upon his disciples.

Here is no outward river: 'He that believeth on me, as the scripture hath said, out of his belly shall flow rivers of living water. But this spake he of the Spirit, which they that believe on him should receive: for the Holy Ghost was not yet given; because that Jesus was not yet glorified', John 7:38,39.

Here are waters not only to the spiritual ankles, but also the knees, rising to the thighs, deepening to waters to swim in: a river of the water of life in which all those who are baptized are spiritually immersed and united.

That is, inwardly. For Jordan was outward, and in those natural waters some half or more of their bodies themselves were immersed, and this could be seen. But the waters of the Holy Ghost cannot be seen, and, invisibly, these fill the spirit and soul of the many baptized therein.

And these things being spiritual—and not natural or visible—neither this spiritual river, nor that baptism of the Spirit, can be seen outwardly or by the carnal sight. Nevertheless, like a mighty flowing river, the one person of the Holy Ghost, issuing forth as the water of life, immerses the members of Christ in the inward man, and fills the hidden man of the heart.

These spiritual waters flow continually into those upon whom they have been shed forth, uniting them in one Spirit, so as to constitute one body, every part as much as—indeed much more than—the figure of Jordan of old flowed about and appeared to unite in one those under John's baptism.

Nevertheless, for all that the baptism of the Spirit from the glorified and heavenly Son is *inward*, so that all are *inwardly* united in one divine person, *this oneness still takes place within their bodies. So that though their spirit and soul is made one, yet their bodies of necessity remain distinct.*

However, within themselves, Christ himself, by the Spirit, fills the one body. Then, *their* bodies signify *his* members. They stand out in that way, as hitherto John's disciples at one and the same time stood in and out of Jordan.

Hence, those baptized in the Holy Ghost are *visibly* one, and *must* be visibly one. 'Know ye not that your *bodies* are the members of Christ?', I Corinthians 6:15.

Christ fills us by the Spirit, who, in turn, himself constituted us inwardly as one body for the indwelling of the Son. Then we *in the wholeness of our being* are his members, and, together, constitute the body of Christ. Just as our own bodies, each one, constitute the outward expression of our own indwelling person and life, so also is the Christ: 'for also in one Spirit are we all baptized into one body.'

And if the baptism with the Holy Ghost is to bring in one body, What is it now? Now it is that *the truth of the one body, of the baptism of the Holy Ghost, has been quite lost, and is, alas, equally unsought, for all the delusions of man and duplications of the Adversary.*

For beyond all shadow of doubt it is evident, *the baptism of the Holy Ghost is corporate, it is to bring into one body. And if this is not the consequence, then what is claimed to be the baptism is not only wholly invalid, it is downright iniquitous, and, at that, in the holy things of the inmost shrine.*

But—as opposed to the imitations of man; the delusions of self-persuasion; the conjuring tricks of hirelings; or, more sinister, the supernatural workings of the Deceiver—the Corinthians, together with all those at the beginning, *really were baptized in one Spirit into one body.*

This was under the ministry of the holy apostle; it was with the power of God; it was of the heavenly glory; it was from the exalted Son of God; it was through the promise of the Father; and it was in the mighty presence and power of the Holy Ghost in the inner man of the assembled believers, that is, *when* they believed.

This made them one, not in themselves alone, but one in the indwelling person of the Holy Ghost. And not one in the indwelling person of the Holy Ghost only, but one in the fulness of him that filleth all in all, so as together to constitute, with all saints—here manifested at Corinth—one body in Christ.

At Corinth? But of old there had been enmity in the city of Corinth; there had been a middle wall of partition at Corinth;

there had been distance betwixt Jew and Gentile at Corinth; the Jews at Corinth would not so much as set foot, let alone sit at meat, with the unclean Gentiles at Corinth.

Then what was this? Out from among the Jews, It was the calling according to the election of grace. Upon the Gentiles great light had arisen in thick heathen darkness, and God had separated the light from the darkness: 'a light to lighten the Gentiles, and the glory of thy people Israel.'

To both Jew and Gentile, God from heaven, the Son from glory, the Spirit on earth, had sent an elect vessel, a chosen apostle, 'to open their eyes, to turn them from darkness to light, and from the power of Satan unto God, that they may receive forgiveness of sins, and inheritance among them which are sanctified by faith that is in me', Acts 26:18.

And now together as one were all baptized in one Spirit into one body.

'Whether we be Jews', to whom first Paul testified that Jesus was Christ, and, when they opposed themselves, called down their blood on their own heads. But Crispus, the chief ruler of the synagogue, and all his house, believed, separating with all other believing Jews from the synagogue.

'Or Gentiles', of whom the Lord said, 'I have much people in this city', and, 'many of the Corinthians believed, and were baptized.'

'Whether we be bond or free'; God is no respecter of persons – though *we*, ourselves, as men, ought to give honour to whom honour is due, which is according to sound doctrine – with God there is no difference, no, neither between bond or free, nor Jew or Gentile, in the like bestowal of this baptism of the Spirit. And so Peter himself testified to the Jews at Jerusalem, 'Forasmuch then as God gave them the like gift as he did unto us, who was I, that I could withstand God?', Acts 11:17.

Yet such a gift to slaves under bondage? But the world's distinctions, whether social or religious, have no place with God. 'Hath not God chosen the poor of this world'–to be–'rich in faith?'

God has chosen us despite our low estate; and the Son knows the elect, and baptizes every one of those whom the Father gave to him; withal, the Spirit is poured out in baptism alike upon all, joining every member together as one–whether Jew or Gentile, bond or free–in the unity of the one body of Christ.

'And have been all made to drink into one Spirit', I Corinthians 12:13. In closing the verse, the apostle employs another illustration. The allegory which he uses now also shows the manner of the union, and, likewise, it is taken from water.

The figure envisaged is that of many who are drinking from one river. They are all drinking into that one river. The river is one, and the water is one. But these men come–not in self-will: they have been *made* to drink!–and all kneel at the river, and all drink.

Now every one has the water of the river within themselves, but, drinking their fill, as they take in the water continually, carrying it dripping from hand to mouth, what is within them is joined in one stream with what they are presently imbibing, which in turn is united with the waters from which they drink.

Thus, in a certain manner, each is joined to the other by what all receive whilst drinking together from the same river.

So it is with spiritualities: with what is of the Spirit. Inwardly our parched souls, made thirsty by the voice of one crying in the wilderness, by the preparatory work of God, cried out for the water that Christ could give, which would satisfy the thirsty soul, giving also to us that fulness–waters to swim in–which we clearly perceived others before us had experienced.

Weeping and crying, in our gasping–'I opened my mouth, and panted', Psalm 119:131–we were like the hart that panteth after the waterbrooks: 'so panteth my soul after thee', Psalm 42:1.

Then, at length, within ourselves sounded the words, 'I will pour water upon him that is thirsty, and floods upon the dry ground', Isaiah 44:3; and thereupon, 'He brought streams also out of the rock, and caused waters to run down like rivers', Psalm 78:16.

The waters came down, they ran down, they descended from 'the river of God, which is full of water', Psalm 65:9, so that he turned our wilderness into a standing water, Psalm 107:35, yea, the rock of our stony hearts into a standing water, the flint of our souls into a fountain of waters, Psalm 114:8.

Hence each one of us could say, and that by experience, 'When the poor and needy seek water, and there is none, and their tongue faileth for thirst, I the LORD will hear them, I the God of Israel will not forsake them. I will open rivers in high places, and fountains in the midst of the valleys: I will make the wilderness a pool of water, and the dry land springs of water', Isaiah 41:17,18.

Therefore have all we been made to drink into one Spirit, I Corinthians 12:13. For Christ having been smitten for us on earth, having justified and redeemed us by his blood, the third day was raised from the dead. Being seen of those witnesses chosen of God, called by the Son as his apostles, after forty days he ascended up into heaven.

Some ten days thereafter, when the day of Pentecost was fully come, there came a sound from heaven as of a rushing mighty wind, and it filled all the house where they were sitting. And there appeared unto them cloven tongues like as of fire, and it sat upon each of them. And they were all filled with the Holy Ghost, and began to speak with other tongues, as the Spirit gave them utterance. And there were dwelling at Jerusalem Jews, devout men, out of every nation under heaven.

Now when this was noised abroad the multitude came together, and were confounded, because every man heard them speak in his own language. Peter declares this to be the fulfilment of Joel's prophecy, the baptism of the Holy Ghost, saying of the Son, 'Therefore being by the right hand of God exalted, and having received of the Father the promise of the Holy Ghost, he hath shed forth this, which ye now see and hear', Acts 2:33.

This is to be baptized with the Holy Ghost. This was the beginning, but there is no ending: the Son baptizes still. This also is to be made to drink into one Spirit which also has no end. For all were, and are, made to drink into that one and the self-same Spirit, in fulfilment of the figure.

For the measure imbibed by each one, as one shed forth upon the whole, fills the one body in union with that divine person who, invisibly and spiritually, unites all in and with himself. And, if so, it follows of course, each is united the one with the other in him, 'for we have *all* been made to drink into one Spirit.' Then, if thus one with him, also united to each other.

Furthermore, we are full, yea, overflowing, because above even such overwhelming blessing as this, the Spirit, flowing from the Father through the Son, joins us in one with the Son.

And not the Son only, for, in the acknowledgement of the fellowship of the mystery, we *experience* that he and his Father are one; then, in the same Spirit, we are united in spirit with the Father through the Son of his love: 'and truly our fellowship is with the Father, and with his Son Jesus Christ', I John 1:3.

This is to 'have all been made to drink'–*drink*–'into'–*into*–'one Spirit', I Corinthians 12:13.

Hence we can echo in our own inward experience the words of Jesus, 'If thou knewest the gift of God, and who it is that saith to thee, Give me to drink; thou wouldest have asked of him, and he would have given thee living water', John 4:10.

For he who slakes his thirst of the water that is in this world must at last cease from drinking. And then he shall thirst again.

'But'–saith Christ–'whosoever drinketh of the water that I shall give him shall never thirst; but the water that I shall give him shall be in him a well of water springing up into everlasting life', John 4:14.

With outward, visible, natural water–that of the world–of necessity one thirsts again in proportion to the length of the period extending from the last time that one drank. Not so with the heavenly, invisible, spiritual water, namely, that of the Son from the glory, in the person of the Holy Ghost.

For this divine, mysterious, heavenly, glorious, spiritual, invisible, and living water, *in its very nature, never has cessation from its outpouring and upspringing, nor do those who receive the gift ever cease to drink therefrom.*

Therefore, they 'never thirst again'. Nor could such spiritual thirst ever be possible, because they have 'all been made to drink into *one Spirit*', I Corinthians 12:13.

Again, such as these cannot but reiterate the words of Jesus, 'If any man thirst, let him come unto me, and drink. He that believeth on me, as the scripture hath said, out of his belly shall flow rivers of living water. But this spake he of the Spirit, which they that believe on him should receive: for the Holy Ghost was not yet given; because that Jesus was not yet glorified', John 7:37-39.

But now he *is* glorified, and, being glorified, it follows, the Spirit has been given. And, if given, then they that believe on the Son must have received him.

This being the case–and from the words of Jesus it must be the case–again it follows of necessity, first, that they have come to him and drank; and, second, that out of their bellies flow rivers of living water.

But then, given the reality of which both drinking and rivers were the figure, this is neither more nor less than that which is written in the event, namely, that they that believe on him 'have all been made to drink into one Spirit', I Corinthians 12:13.

And what is this?

This is *none other—given the unity of the deity in Father, Son, and Holy Ghost—none other than* 'As thou, Father, art in me, and I in thee, that they also may be one in us', *John 17:21.*

JOHN METCALFE

INDEX

TO OTHER PUBLICATIONS

PSALMS, HYMNS AND SPIRITUAL SONGS

THE PSALMS

OF THE

OLD TESTAMENT

The Psalms of the Old Testament, the result of years of painstaking labour, is an original translation into verse from the Authorized Version, which seeks to present the Psalms in the purest scriptural form possible for singing. Here, for the first time, divine names are rendered as and when they occur in the scripture, the distinction between LORD and Lord has been preserved, and every essential point of doctrine and experience appears with unique perception and fidelity.

The Psalms of the Old Testament is the first part of a trilogy written by John Metcalfe, the second part of which is entitled *Spiritual Songs from the Gospels*, and the last, *The Hymns of the New Testament*. These titles provide unique and accurate metrical versions of passages from the psalms, the gospels and the new testament epistles respectively, and are intended to be used together in the worship of God.

Price £2.50 (*postage extra*)
(hard-case binding, dust-jacket)
Printed, sewn and bound
by the John Metcalfe Publishing Trust
ISBN 1 870039 75 0

SPIRITUAL SONGS

FROM

THE GOSPELS

The *Spiritual Songs from the Gospels*, the result of years of painstaking labour, is an original translation into verse from the Authorized Version, which seeks to present essential parts of the gospels in the purest scriptural form possible for singing. The careful selection from Matthew, Mark, Luke, and John, set forth in metrical verse of the highest integrity, enables the singer to sing 'the word of Christ' as if from the scripture itself, 'richly and in all wisdom'; and, above all, in a way that facilitates worship in song of unprecedented fidelity.

The *Spiritual Songs from the Gospels* is the central part of a trilogy written by John Metcalfe, the first part of which is entitled *The Psalms of the Old Testament*, and the last, *The Hymns of the New Testament*. These titles provide unique and accurate metrical versions of passages from the psalms, the gospels and the new testament epistles respectively, and are intended to be used together in the worship of God.

Price £2.50 *(postage extra)*
(hard-case binding, dust-jacket)
Printed, sewn and bound
by the John Metcalfe Publishing Trust
ISBN 0 9506366 8 1

THE HYMNS

OF THE

NEW TESTAMENT

The Hymns of the New Testament, the result of years of painstaking labour, is an original translation into verse from the Authorized Version, which presents essential parts of the new testament epistles in the purest scriptural form possible for singing. The careful selection from the book of Acts to that of Revelation, set forth in metrical verse of the highest integrity, enables the singer to sing 'the word of Christ' as if from the scripture itself, 'richly and in all wisdom'; and, above all, in a way that facilitates worship in song of unprecedented fidelity.

The Hymns of the New Testament is the last part of a trilogy written by John Metcalfe, the first part of which is entitled *The Psalms of the Old Testament*, and the next, *Spiritual Songs from the Gospels*. These titles provide unique and accurate metrical versions of passages from the psalms, the gospels and the new testament epistles respectively, and are intended to be used together in the worship of God.

Price £2.50 *(postage extra)*
(hard-case binding, dust-jacket)
Printed, sewn and bound
by the John Metcalfe Publishing Trust
ISBN 0 9506366 9 X

'THE APOSTOLIC FOUNDATION
OF THE
CHRISTIAN CHURCH' SERIES

Third Printing

FOUNDATIONS UNCOVERED

THE APOSTOLIC FOUNDATION
OF THE
CHRISTIAN CHURCH

Volume I

Foundations Uncovered is the introduction to the major series: 'The Apostolic Foundation of the Christian Church'.

Rich in truth, the Introduction deals comprehensively with the foundation of the apostolic faith under the descriptive titles: The Word, The Doctrine, The Truth, The Gospel, The Faith, The New Testament, and The Foundation.

The contents of the book reveal: The Fact of the Foundation; The Foundation Uncovered; What the Foundation is not; How the Foundation is Described; and, Being Built upon the Foundation.

'This book comes with the freshness of a new Reformation.'

Price 75p *(postage extra)*
Paperback 110 pages (Laminated cover)
Printed, sewn and bound
by the John Metcalfe Publishing Trust
ISBN 0 9506366 5 7

Thoroughly revised and extensively rewritten
second edition

Third Printing

THE BIRTH OF JESUS CHRIST

THE APOSTOLIC FOUNDATION
OF THE
CHRISTIAN CHURCH

Volume II

'The very spirit of adoration and worship rings through the pages of *The Birth of Jesus Christ*.

'The author expresses with great clarity the truths revealed to him in his study of holy scriptures at depth. We are presented here with a totally lofty view of the Incarnation.

'John Metcalfe is to be classed amongst the foremost expositors of our age; and his writings have about them that quality of timelessness that makes me sure they will one day take their place among the heritage of truly great Christian works.'

From a review by Rev. David Catterson.

'Uncompromisingly faithful to scripture ... has much to offer which is worth serious consideration ... deeply moving.'

The Expository Times.

Price 95p *(postage extra)*
Paperback 160 pages (Laminated cover)
Printed, sewn and bound
by the John Metcalfe Publishing Trust
ISBN 1 870039 48 3

Thoroughly revised and extensively rewritten
second edition (Hardback)

Third Printing

THE MESSIAH

THE APOSTOLIC FOUNDATION
OF THE
CHRISTIAN CHURCH

Volume III

The Messiah is a spiritually penetrating and entirely original exposition of Matthew chapter one to chapter seven from the trenchant pen of John Metcalfe.

Matthew Chapters One to Seven

GENEALOGY · BIRTH · STAR OF BETHLEHEM
HEROD · FLIGHT TO EGYPT · NAZARETH
JOHN THE BAPTIST · THE BAPTIST'S MINISTRY
JESUS' BAPTISM · ALL RIGHTEOUSNESS FULFILLED
HEAVEN OPENED · THE SPIRIT'S DESCENT
THE TEMPTATION OF JESUS IN THE WILDERNESS
JESUS' MANIFESTATION · THE CALLING · THE TRUE DISCIPLES
THE BEATITUDES · THE SERMON ON THE MOUNT

'Something of the fire of the ancient Hebrew prophet ......
Metcalfe has spiritual and expository potentials of a high order.'
The Life of Faith.

Price £7.75 *(postage extra)*
Hardback 420 pages
Laminated bookjacket
Printed, sewn and bound
by the John Metcalfe Publishing Trust
ISBN 1 870039 51 3

Second Edition (Hardback)

THE SON OF GOD AND SEED OF DAVID

THE APOSTOLIC FOUNDATION
OF THE
CHRISTIAN CHURCH

Volume IV

The Son of God and Seed of David is the fourth volume in the major work entitled 'The Apostolic Foundation of the Christian Church'.

'The Author proceeds to open and allege that Jesus Christ is and ever was *The Son of God*. This greatest of subjects, this most profound of all mysteries, is handled with reverence and with outstanding perception.

'The second part considers *The Seed of David*. What is meant precisely by 'the seed'? And why 'of David'? With prophetic insight the author expounds these essential verities.

Price £6.95 *(postage extra)*
Hardback 250 pages
Laminated bookjacket
Printed, sewn and bound
by the John Metcalfe Publishing Trust
ISBN 1 870039 16 5

CHRIST CRUCIFIED

THE APOSTOLIC FOUNDATION
OF THE
CHRISTIAN CHURCH

Volume V

Christ Crucified, the definitive work on the crucifixion, the blood, and the cross of Jesus Christ.

The crucifixion of Jesus Christ witnessed in the Gospels: the gospel according to Matthew; Mark; Luke; John.

The blood of Jesus Christ declared in the Epistles: the shed blood; the blood of purchase; redemption through his blood; the blood of sprinkling; the blood of the covenant.

The doctrine of the cross revealed in the apostolic foundation of the Christian church: the doctrine of the cross; the cross and the body of sin; the cross and the carnal mind; the cross and the law; the offence of the cross; the cross of our Lord Jesus Christ.

Price £6.95 *(postage extra)*
Hardback 300 pages
Laminated bookjacket
Printed, sewn and bound
by the John Metcalfe Publishing Trust
ISBN 1 870039 08 4

JUSTIFICATION BY FAITH

THE APOSTOLIC FOUNDATION
OF THE
CHRISTIAN CHURCH

Volume VI

THE HEART OF THE GOSPEL · THE FOUNDATION OF THE CHURCH
THE ISSUE OF ETERNITY
CLEARLY, ORIGINALLY AND POWERFULLY OPENED

The basis · The righteousness of the law
The righteousness of God · The atonement · Justification
Traditional views considered · Righteousness imputed to faith
Faith counted for righteousness · Justification by Faith

'And it came to pass, when Jesus had ended these sayings, the people
were astonished at his doctrine: for he taught them as one having
authority, and not as the scribes', Matthew 7:28,29.

Price £7.50 (postage extra)
Hardback 375 pages
Laminated bookjacket
Printed, sewn and bound
by the John Metcalfe Publishing Trust
ISBN 1 870039 11 4

THE CHURCH: WHAT IS IT?

THE APOSTOLIC FOUNDATION
OF THE
CHRISTIAN CHURCH

Volume VII

The answer to this question proceeds first from the lips of Jesus himself, Mt. 16:18, later to be expounded by the words of the apostles whom he sent.

Neither fear of man nor favour from the world remotely affect the answer.

Here is the truth, the whole truth, and nothing but the truth.

The complete originality, the vast range, and the total fearlessness of this book command the attention in a way that is unique.

Read this book: you will never read another like it.

Outspokenly devastating yet devastatingly constructive.

Price £7.75 *(postage extra)*
Hardback 400 pages
Laminated bookjacket
Printed, sewn and bound
by the John Metcalfe Publishing Trust
ISBN 1 870039 23 8

THE REVELATION OF JESUS CHRIST

THE APOSTOLIC FOUNDATION
OF THE
CHRISTIAN CHURCH

Volume VIII

Uniquely perceptive and original, the result of decades alone in the secret place of the most High, abiding under the shadow of the Almighty, this peerless work on the Revelation of Jesus Christ will stand the test of time and eternity for its heavenly, spiritual, and divine opening into the last book of the last apostle of the new testament, for all who have an ear to hear what the Spirit saith unto the churches.

Here is the transcript of the series of addresses delivered over some eighteen months during 1997 and 1998, in the Assembly Hall, Church House, Westminster, London, by John Metcalfe.

The famed Assembly Hall is used as the Synod Chamber of the Church of England as occasion requires.

Price £9.25 (*postage extra*)
Hardback 640 pages
Laminated bookjacket
Printed, sewn and bound
by the John Metcalfe Publishing Trust
ISBN 1 870039 77 7

LECTURES
FROM
CHURCH HOUSE, WESTMINSTER

COLOSSIANS

This concise and unique revelation of the Epistle to the Colossians has the hallmark of spiritual originality and insight peculiar to the ministry of John Metcalfe. It is as if a diamond, inert and lifeless in itself, has been divinely cut at great cost, so that every way in which it is turned, the light from above is enhanced and magnified to break forth with divine radiance showing colour and depth hitherto unsuspected.

Price 95p (*postage extra*)
Paperback 135 pages (Laminated cover)
Printed, sewn and bound
by the John Metcalfe Publishing Trust
ISBN 1 870039 55 6

MATTHEW

This concise revelation of the essence and structure of the Gospel according to Matthew, the culmination of years of prayer and devotion, retreat and study, opens the mind of the Spirit in the unique vision of Jesus Christ, the son of David, the son of Abraham, recorded in the first gospel.

Price 95p (*postage extra*)
Paperback 135 pages (Laminated cover)
Printed, sewn and bound
by the John Metcalfe Publishing Trust
ISBN 1 870039 61 0

PHILIPPIANS

The Epistle of Paul the Apostle to the Philippians is opened by this work from the pen of John Metcalfe with that lucid thoroughness which one has come to expect from a ministry received 'not of men, neither by man, but by the revelation of Jesus Christ'.

The work of God at Philippi is traced 'from the first day' until the time at which the epistle was written. Never was Lydia or the Philippian jailor drawn with more lively insight. The epistle itself is revealed in order, with passages–such as 'the mind that was in Christ Jesus'–that evidence the work of no less than a divine for our own times.

Price £1.90 (*postage extra*)
Paperback 185 pages (Laminated cover)
Printed, sewn and bound
by the John Metcalfe Publishing Trust
ISBN 1 870039 56 4

PHILEMON

This penetrating revelation of the Epistle to Philemon opens the substance of four consecutive lectures given by John Metcalfe in The Hoare Memorial Hall, Church House, Westminster, London.

Price £1.90 (*postage extra*)
Paperback 190 pages (Laminated cover)
Printed, sewn and bound
by the John Metcalfe Publishing Trust
ISBN 1 870039 66 1

FIRST TIMOTHY

This penetrating revelation of the First Epistle to Timothy opens the substance of five consecutive lectures given by John Metcalfe in The Hoare Memorial Hall, Church House, Westminster, London.

Price £2.00 (*postage extra*)
Paperback 220 pages (Laminated cover)
Printed, sewn and bound
by the John Metcalfe Publishing Trust
ISBN 1 870039 67 X

MARK

This penetrating revelation of the Gospel according to Mark opens the substance of seven consecutive lectures given by John Metcalfe in The Hoare Memorial Hall, Church House, Westminster, London.

Price £2.35 (*postage extra*)
Paperback 290 pages (Laminated cover)
Printed, sewn and bound
by the John Metcalfe Publishing Trust
ISBN 1 870039 70 X

CREATION

Genesis 1:1, 'In the beginning God created the heaven and the earth.'

This spiritually penetrating and outstandingly original revelation of the Creation from Genesis chapters 1 and 2 opens the substance of five consecutive lectures given by John Metcalfe, commencing in the Hoare Memorial Hall and later moving to the central Assembly Hall, Church House, Westminster, London.

The Hoare Memorial Hall was used as the House of Commons at various times during the Second World War. Many of Sir Winston Churchill's renowned war time speeches were delivered in this Hall.

The famed Assembly Hall is used as the Synod Chamber of the Church of England as occasion requires.

Price £2.00 (*postage extra*)
Paperback 230 pages (Laminated cover)
Printed, sewn and bound
by the John Metcalfe Publishing Trust
ISBN 1 870039 71 8

NEWLY PUBLISHED

THE FIRST EPISTLE OF JOHN

Deeply spiritual and of the very essence, it is as if one heard the apostle himself taking and opening the book in a way that is unprecedented.

THE BEGINNING . THE MESSAGE . THE COMMANDMENTS
THE LITTLE CHILDREN . THE ABIDING
THE WITNESS . THE CONCLUSION

Price £9.25 (*postage extra*)
Hardback 585 pages
Laminated bookjacket
Printed, sewn and bound
by the John Metcalfe Publishing Trust
ISBN 1 870039 78 5

OTHER TITLES

NOAH AND THE FLOOD

Noah and the Flood expounds with vital urgency the man and the message that heralded the end of the old world. The description of the flood itself is vividly realistic. The whole work has an unmistakable ring of authority, and speaks as 'Thus saith the Lord'.

'Mr. Metcalfe makes a skilful use of persuasive eloquence as he challenges the reality of one's profession of faith ... he gives a rousing call to a searching self-examination and evaluation of one's spiritual experience.'

The Monthly Record of the Free Church of Scotland.

Price £1.90 *(postage extra)*
Paperback 155 pages (Laminated cover)
Printed, sewn and bound
by the John Metcalfe Publishing Trust
ISBN 1 870039 22 X

DIVINE FOOTSTEPS

Divine Footsteps traces the pathway of the feet of the Son of man from the very beginning in the prophetic figures of the true in the old testament through the reality in the new; doing so in a way of experimental spirituality. At the last a glimpse of the coming glory is beheld as his feet are viewed as standing at the latter day upon the earth.

Price 95p *(postage extra)*
Paperback 120 pages (Laminated cover)
Printed, sewn and bound by
the John Metcalfe Publishing Trust
ISBN 1 870039 21 1

THE RED HEIFER

The Red Heifer was the name given to a sacrifice used by the children of Israel in the Old Testament – as recorded in Numbers 19 – in which a heifer was slain and burned. Cedar wood, hyssop and scarlet were cast into the burning, and the ashes were mingled with running water and put in a vessel. It was kept for the children of Israel for a water of separation: it was a purification for sin.

In this unusual book the sacrifice is brought up to date and its relevance to the church today is shown.

Price 75p *(postage extra)*
Paperback 100 pages
ISBN 0 9502515 4 2

OF GOD OR MAN?

LIGHT FROM GALATIANS

The Epistle to the Galatians contends for deliverance from the law and from carnal ministry.

The Apostle opens his matter in two ways:

Firstly, Paul vindicates himself and his ministry against those that came not from God above, but from Jerusalem below.

Secondly, he defends the Gospel and evangelical liberty against legal perversions and bondage to the flesh.

Price £1.45 *(postage extra)*
Paperback 190 pages (Laminated cover)
ISBN 0 9506366 3 0

THE BOOK OF RUTH

The Book of Ruth is set against the farming background of old testament Israel at the time of the Judges, the narrative – unfolding the work of God in redemption–being marked by a series of agricultural events.

These events–the famine; the barley harvest; the wheat harvest; the winnowing–possessed a hidden spiritual significance to that community, but, much more, they speak in figure directly to our own times, as the book reveals.

Equally contemporary appear the characters of Ruth, Naomi, Boaz, and the first kinsman, drawn with spiritual perception greatly to the profit of the reader.

Price £4.95 (*postage extra*)
Hardback 200 pages
Laminated bookjacket
Printed, sewn and bound
by the John Metcalfe Publishing Trust
ISBN 1 870039 17 3

A QUESTION FOR POPE JOHN PAUL II

As a consequence of his many years spent apart in prayer, lonely vigil, and painstaking study of the scripture, John Metcalfe asks a question and looks for an answer from Pope John Paul II.

Price £1.25 (*postage extra*)
Paperback 105 pages (Laminated cover)
ISBN 0 9506366 4 9

DIVINE MEDITATIONS

OF

WILLIAM HUNTINGTON

Originally published by Mr. Huntington as a series of letters to J. Jenkins, under the title of 'Contemplations on the God of Israel', the spiritual content of this correspondence has been skilfully and sympathetically edited, abridged, and arranged so as to form a series of meditations, suitable for daily readings.

Mr. Huntington's own text is thereby adapted to speak directly to the reader in a way much more suited to his ministering immediately to ourselves, in our own circumstances and times.

It is greatly hoped that many today will benefit from this adaption which carefully retains both the spirit and the letter of the text. If any prefer the original format, this is readily available from several sources and many libraries.

Nevertheless, the publishers believe the much more readable form into which Mr. Huntington's very words have been adapted will appeal to a far wider audience, for whose comfort and consolation this carefully edited work has been published.

Price £2.35 (postage extra)
Paperback 300 pages (Laminated cover)
Printed, sewn and bound
by the John Metcalfe Publishing Trust
ISBN 1 870039 24 6

Second Edition

Third Printing

THE WELLS OF SALVATION

The Wells of Salvation is written from a series of seven powerful addresses preached at Tylers Green. It is a forthright and experimental exposition of Isaiah 12:3, 'Therefore with joy shall ye draw water out of the wells of salvation.'

John Metcalfe is acknowledged to be perhaps the most gifted expositor and powerful preacher of our day and this is to be seen clearly in The Wells of Salvation.

Price £2.35 (*postage extra*)
Paperback 285 pages (Laminated cover)
Printed, sewn and bound
by the John Metcalfe Publishing Trust
ISBN 1 870039 72 6

Second Printing

SAVING FAITH

The sevenfold work of the Holy Ghost in bringing a sinner to saving faith in Christ opened and enlarged.

True faith is the work of God. False faith is the presumption of man. But where is the difference? *Saving Faith* shows the difference.

Price £2.25 (*postage extra*)
Paperback 250 pages (Laminated cover)
Printed, sewn and bound
by the John Metcalfe Publishing Trust
ISBN 1 870039 40 8

DELIVERANCE FROM THE LAW
THE WESTMINSTER CONFESSION EXPLODED

Deliverance from the Law. A devastating vindication of the gospel of Christ against the traditions of man.

Price £1.90 (*postage extra*)
Paperback 160 pages (Laminated cover)
Printed, sewn and bound
by the John Metcalfe Publishing Trust
ISBN 1 870039 41 6

PRESENT-DAY CONVERSIONS
OF THE NEW TESTAMENT KIND

FROM THE MINISTRY OF
JOHN METCALFE

The outstandingly striking presentation of this fascinating paperback will surely catch the eye, as its title and contents will certainly captivate the mind: here is a unique publication.

Woven into a gripping narrative, over twenty-one short life stories, all centred on conversions that simply could not have happened had not God broken in, and had not Christ been revealed, the book presents a tremendous challenge, at once moving and thrilling to the reader.

Price £2.25 (*postage extra*)
Paperback 240 pages (Laminated cover)
Printed, sewn and bound
by the John Metcalfe Publishing Trust
ISBN 1 870039 31 9

THE BEATITUDES

A unique insight destined to be the classic opening of this wonderful sequence of utterances from the lips of Jesus.

The reader will discover a penetration of the spiritual heights and divine depths of these peerless words in a way ever fresh and always rewarding though read time and time again.

Price £1.90 (*postage extra*)
Paperback 185 pages (Laminated cover)
Printed, sewn and bound
by the John Metcalfe Publishing Trust
ISBN 1 870039 45 9

PASTORAL LETTERS TO THE FAR EAST

Feeling the abiding spiritual value of letters written by John Metcalfe in his absence from the Far East, Miss Sie Siok Hui cherished the correspondence to her, and at the same time was moved to seek for similar writings to some of her closest sisters in Christ.

Gathering these letters together, it was her earnest desire that such an enduring testimony should be made available to all the faithful remnant in our own day. The result of her prayers and spiritual exercise appears in the publication 'Pastoral Letters to the Far East'.

Price £2.00 (*postage extra*)
Paperback 240 pages (Laminated cover)
Printed, sewn and bound
by the John Metcalfe Publishing Trust
ISBN 1 870039 74 2

LAW AND GRACE CONTRASTED

A SERIES OF ADDRESSES

BY

WILLIAM HUNTINGTON

The Child of Liberty in Legal Bondage · The Bondchild
brought to the Test · The Modern Plasterer Detected
Not under Law · The Law a Rule of Life?

Mr. Huntington's own text is adapted to speak directly to the
reader in a way much more suited to his ministering immediately to ourselves, in our own circumstances and times.

It is greatly hoped that many today will benefit from this
adaption which carefully retains both the spirit and the letter
of the text. If any prefer the original format, this is readily
available from several sources and many libraries.

Nevertheless, the publishers believe the much more readable
form into which Mr. Huntington's very words have been
adapted will appeal to a far wider audience, for whose comfort
and consolation this carefully edited work has been published.

Price £2.35 (*postage extra*)
Paperback 265 pages (Laminated cover)
Printed, sewn and bound
by the John Metcalfe Publishing Trust
ISBN 1 870039 76 9

NEWLY PUBLISHED

THE BODY OF CHRIST AND THE GIFTS

For so long confusion has reigned in respect of THE BODY OF CHRIST AND THE GIFTS. Here at last is that spiritual, sound, and balanced opening of the Holy Scripture from I Corinthians 12:14-13:13.

This gives the unmistakable ring of apostolic authority, puts the matter beyond the realm of speculation or experiment, past all doubt bringing the text into the light of revelation of Jesus Christ.

Price 95p (*postage extra*)
Paperback 140 pages (Laminated cover)
Printed, sewn and bound
by the John Metcalfe Publishing Trust
ISBN 1 870039 82 3

'TRACT FOR THE TIMES' SERIES

'TRACT FOR THE TIMES' SERIES

The Gospel of God by John Metcalfe. No. 1 in the Series. Laminated cover, price 25p.

The Strait Gate by John Metcalfe. No. 2 in the Series. Laminated cover, price 25p.

Eternal Sonship and Taylor Brethren by John Metcalfe. No. 3 in the Series. Laminated cover, price 25p.

Marks of the New Testament Church by John Metcalfe. No. 4 in the Series. Laminated cover, price 25p.

The Charismatic Delusion by John Metcalfe. No. 5 in the Series. Laminated cover, price 25p.

Premillennialism Exposed by John Metcalfe. No. 6 in the Series. Laminated cover, price 25p.

Justification and Peace by John Metcalfe. No. 7 in the Series. Laminated cover, price 25p.

Faith or Presumption? by John Metcalfe. No. 8 in the Series. Laminated cover, price 25p.

The Elect Undeceived by John Metcalfe. No. 9 in the Series. Laminated cover, price 25p.

Justifying Righteousness by John Metcalfe. No. 10 in the Series. Laminated cover, price 25p.

Righteousness Imputed by John Metcalfe. No. 11 in the Series. Laminated cover, price 25p.

The Great Deception by John Metcalfe. No. 12 in the Series. Laminated cover, price 25p.

A Famine in the Land by John Metcalfe. No. 13 in the Series. Laminated cover, price 25p.

Blood and Water by John Metcalfe. No. 14 in the Series. Laminated cover, price 25p.

Women Bishops? by John Metcalfe. No. 15 in the Series. Laminated cover, price 25p.

The Heavenly Vision by John Metcalfe. No. 16 in the Series. Laminated cover, price 25p.

EVANGELICAL TRACTS

EVANGELICAL TRACTS

1. **The Two Prayers of Elijah.** Light green card cover, price 10p.

2. **Wounded for our Transgressions.** Gold card cover, price 10p.

3. **The Blood of Sprinkling.** Red card cover, price 10p.

4. **The Grace of God that brings Salvation.** Blue card cover, price 10p.

5. **The Name of Jesus.** Rose card cover, price 10p.

6. **The Ministry of the New Testament.** Purple card cover, price 10p.

7. **The Death of the Righteous** (*The closing days of J.B. Stoney*) by A.M.S. (his daughter). Ivory card cover, price 10p.

8. **Repentance.** Sky blue card cover, price 10p.

9. **Legal Deceivers Exposed.** Crimson card cover, price 10p.

10. **Unconditional Salvation.** Green card cover, price 10p.

11. **Religious Merchandise.** Brown card cover, price 10p.

12. **Comfort.** Pink card cover, price 10p.

13. **Peace.** Grey card cover, price 10p.

14. **Eternal Life.** Cobalt card cover, price 10p.

15. **The Handwriting of Ordinances.** Fawn card cover, price 10p.

16. **'Lord, Lord!'.** Emerald card cover, price 10p.

17. **Conversion.** Wedgewood card cover, price 10p.

ECCLESIA TRACTS

ECCLESIA TRACTS

The Beginning of the Ecclesia by John Metcalfe. No. 1 in the Series, Sand grain cover, price 10p.

Churches and the Church by J.N. Darby. Edited. No. 2 in the Series, Sand grain cover, price 10p.

The Ministers of Christ by John Metcalfe. No. 3 in the Series, Sand grain cover, price 10p.

The Inward Witness by George Fox. Edited. No. 4 in the Series, Sand grain cover, price 10p.

The Notion of a Clergyman by J.N. Darby. Edited. No. 5 in the Series, Sand grain cover, price 10p.

The Servant of the Lord by William Huntington. Edited and Abridged. No. 6 in the Series, Sand grain cover, price 10p.

One Spirit by William Kelly. Edited. No. 7 in the Series, Sand grain cover, price 10p.

The Funeral of Arminianism by William Huntington. Edited and Abridged. No. 8 in the Series, Sand grain cover, price 10p.

One Body by William Kelly. Edited. No. 9 in the Series, Sand grain cover, price 10p.

False Churches and True by John Metcalfe. No. 10 in the Series, Sand grain cover, price 10p.

Separation from Evil by J.N. Darby. Edited. No. 11 in the Series, Sand grain cover, price 10p.

The Remnant by J.B. Stoney. Edited. No. 12 in the Series, Sand grain cover, price 10p.

The Arminian Skeleton by William Huntington. Edited and Abridged. No. 13 in the Series, Sand grain cover, price 10p.

1

FOUNDATION TRACTS

FOUNDATION TRACTS

1. **Female Priests?** by John Metcalfe. Oatmeal cover, price 25p.

2. **The Bondage of the Will** by Martin Luther. Translated and Abridged. Oatmeal cover, price 25p.

3. **Of the Popish Mass** by John Calvin. Translated and Abridged. Oatmeal cover, price 25p.

4. **The Adversary** by John Metcalfe. Oatmeal cover, price 25p.

5. **The Advance of Popery** by J.C. Philpot. Oatmeal cover, price 25p.

6. **Enemies in the Land** by John Metcalfe. Oatmeal cover, price 25p.

7. **An Admonition Concerning Relics** by John Calvin. Oatmeal cover, price 25p.

8. **John Metcalfe's Testimony Against Falsity in Worship** by John Metcalfe. Oatmeal cover, price 25p.

9. **Brethrenism Exposed** by John Metcalfe. Oatmeal cover, price 25p.

10. **John Metcalfe's Testimony Against The Social Gospel** by John Metcalfe. Oatmeal cover, price 25p.

MINISTRY BY JOHN METCALFE

TAPE MINISTRY BY JOHN METCALFE
FROM THE U.K. AND THE FAR EAST
IS AVAILABLE

In order to obtain this free recorded ministry, please send your blank cassette (C.90) and the cost of the return postage, including your name and address in block capitals, to the John Metcalfe Publishing Trust, Church Road, Tylers Green, Penn, Bucks, HP10 8LN. Tapelists are available on request.

Owing to the increased demand for the tape ministry, we are unable to supply more than two tapes per order, except in the case of meetings for the hearing of tapes, where a special arrangement can be made.

THE MINISTRY OF THE NEW TESTAMENT

The purpose of this substantial A4 gloss paper magazine is to provide spiritual and experimental ministry with sound doctrine which rightly and prophetically divides the word of truth.

Readers of our books will already know the high standards of our publications. They can be confident that these pages will maintain that quality, by giving access to enduring ministry from the past, much of which is derived from sources that are virtually unobtainable today, and publishing a living ministry from the present. Selected articles from the following writers have already been included:

ELI ASHDOWN · JOHN BERRIDGE · ABRAHAM BOOTH
JOHN BRADFORD · JOHN BUNYAN · JOHN BURGON
JOHN CALVIN · DONALD CARGILL · JOHN CENNICK · J.N. DARBY
GEORGE FOX · JOHN FOXE · WILLIAM GADSBY · JOHN GUTHRIE
WILLIAM GUTHRIE · GREY HAZLERIGG · WILLIAM HUNTINGTON
WILLIAM KELLY · JOHN KENNEDY · JOHN KERSHAW
JOHN KEYT · HANSERD KNOLLYS · JOHN KNOX · JAMES LEWIS
MARTIN LUTHER · ROBERT MURRAY MCCHEYNE · JOHN METCALFE
BROWNLOW NORTH · THOMAS OXENHAM · ALEXANDER–SANDY–PEDEN
J.C. PHILPOT · J.K. POPHAM · JAMES RENWICK · J.B. STONEY
HENRY TANNER · ARTHUR TRIGGS · JOHN VINALL · JOHN WARBURTON
JOHN WELWOOD · GEORGE WHITEFIELD · J.A. WYLIE

Price £1.75 (*postage included*)
Issued Spring, Summer, Autumn, Winter.

Magazine Order Form

Name and address (in block capitals)

....

....

....

cut here

Please send me ...... current copy/copies of The Ministry of the New Testament.

Please send me ...... year/s subscription.

I enclose a cheque/postal order for £......

(Price: including postage, U.K. £1.75; Overseas £1.90)
(One year's subscription: including postage, U.K. £7.00; Overseas £7.60)

Cheques should be made payable to The John Metcalfe Publishing Trust, and for overseas subscribers should be in pounds sterling drawn on a London Bank.

10 or more copies to one address will qualify for a 10% discount.

Some back numbers from Spring 1986 available.

Please send to The John Metcalfe Publishing Trust, Church Road, Tylers Green, Penn, Bucks, HP10 8LN.

All publications of the Trust are subsidised by the Publishers

lvii

Book Order Form

Please send to the address below:

	Price	Quantity
A Question for Pope John Paul II	£1.25	......
Of God or Man?	£1.45	......
Noah and the Flood	£1.90	......
Divine Footsteps	£0.95	......
The Red Heifer	£0.75	......
The Wells of Salvation	£2.35	......
The Book of Ruth (Hardback edition)	£4.95	......
Divine Meditations of William Huntington	£2.35	......
Present-Day Conversions of the New Testament Kind	£2.25	......
Saving Faith	£2.25	......
Deliverance from the Law	£1.90	......
The Beatitudes	£1.90	......
Pastoral Letters to the Far East	£2.00	......
Law and Grace Contrasted by William Huntington	£2.35	......
The Gifts and Baptism of the Spirit	£0.95	......
The Body of Christ and the Gifts	£0.95	......

Lectures from Church House, Westminster

	Price	Quantity
Colossians	£0.95	......
Philippians	£1.90	......
Matthew	£0.95	......
Philemon	£1.90	......
First Timothy	£2.00	......
Mark	£2.35	......
Creation	£2.00	......
The First Epistle of John (Hardback edition)	£9.25	......

Psalms, Hymns & Spiritual Songs (Hardback edition)

	Price	Quantity
The Psalms of the Old Testament	£2.50	......
Spiritual Songs from the Gospels	£2.50	......
The Hymns of the New Testament	£2.50	......

'Apostolic Foundation of the Christian Church' series

		Price	Quantity
Foundations Uncovered	Vol. I	£0.75	......
The Birth of Jesus Christ	Vol. II	£0.95	......
The Messiah (Hardback edition)	Vol. III	£7.75	......
The Son of God and Seed of David (Hardback edition)	Vol. IV	£6.95	......
Christ Crucified (Hardback edition)	Vol. V	£6.95	......
Justification by Faith (Hardback edition)	Vol. VI	£7.50	......
The Church: What is it? (Hardback edition)	Vol. VII	£7.75	......
The Revelation of Jesus Christ (Hardback edition)	Vol. VIII	£9.25	......

Name and address (in block capitals)

....

....

....

If money is sent with order please allow for postage. Please address to:- The John Metcalfe Publishing Trust, Church Road, Tylers Green, Penn, Bucks, HP10 8LN.

cut here

Tract Order Form

Please send to the address below:

		Price	Quantity
Evangelical Tracts			
The Two Prayers of Elijah		£0.10	......
Wounded for our Transgressions		£0.10	......
The Blood of Sprinkling		£0.10	......
The Grace of God that brings Salvation		£0.10	......
The Name of Jesus		£0.10	......
The Ministry of the New Testament		£0.10	......
The Death of the Righteous by A.M.S.		£0.10	......
Repentance		£0.10	......
Legal Deceivers Exposed		£0.10	......
Unconditional Salvation		£0.10	......
Religious Merchandise		£0.10	......
Comfort		£0.10	......
Peace		£0.10	......
Eternal Life		£0.10	......
The Handwriting of Ordinances		£0.10	......
'Lord, Lord!'		£0.10	......
Conversion		£0.10	......
'Tract for the Times' series			
The Gospel of God	No. 1	£0.25	......
The Strait Gate	No. 2	£0.25	......
Eternal Sonship and Taylor Brethren	No. 3	£0.25	......
Marks of the New Testament Church	No. 4	£0.25	......
The Charismatic Delusion	No. 5	£0.25	......
Premillennialism Exposed	No. 6	£0.25	......
Justification and Peace	No. 7	£0.25	......
Faith or Presumption?	No. 8	£0.25	......
The Elect Undeceived	No. 9	£0.25	......
Justifying Righteousness	No.10	£0.25	......
Righteousness Imputed	No.11	£0.25	......
The Great Deception	No.12	£0.25	......
A Famine in the Land	No.13	£0.25	......
Blood and Water	No.14	£0.25	......
Women Bishops?	No.15	£0.25	......
The Heavenly Vision	No.16	£0.25	......

Name and address (in block capitals)

....

....

....

If money is sent with order please allow for postage. Please address to:- The
John Metcalfe Publishing Trust, Church Road, Tylers Green, Penn, Bucks, HP10 8LN.

cut here

Tract Order Form

Please send to the address below:

	Price	Quantity

Ecclesia Tracts

		Price	Quantity
The Beginning of the Ecclesia	No. 1	£0.10	......
Churches and the Church (J.N.D.)	No. 2	£0.10	......
The Ministers of Christ	No. 3	£0.10	......
The Inward Witness (G.F.)	No. 4	£0.10	......
The Notion of a Clergyman (J.N.D.)	No. 5	£0.10	......
The Servant of the Lord (W.H.)	No. 6	£0.10	......
One Spirit (W.K.)	No. 7	£0.10	......
The Funeral of Arminianism (W.H.)	No. 8	£0.10	......
One Body (W.K.)	No. 9	£0.10	......
False Churches and True	No.10	£0.10	......
Separation from Evil (J.N.D.)	No.11	£0.10	......
The Remnant (J.B.S.)	No.12	£0.10	......
The Arminian Skeleton (W.H.)	No.13	£0.10	......

Foundation Tracts

		Price	Quantity
Female Priests?	No. 1	£0.25	......
The Bondage of the Will (Martin Luther)	No. 2	£0.25	......
Of the Popish Mass (John Calvin)	No. 3	£0.25	......
The Adversary	No. 4	£0.25	......
The Advance of Popery (J.C. Philpot)	No. 5	£0.25	......
Enemies in the Land	No. 6	£0.25	......
An Admonition Concerning Relics (John Calvin)	No. 7	£0.25	......
John Metcalfe's Testimony Against Falsity in Worship	No. 8	£0.25	......
Brethrenism Exposed	No. 9	£0.25	......
John Metcalfe's Testimony Against The Social Gospel	No.10	£0.25	......

Name and address (in block capitals)

....

....

....

If money is sent with order please allow for postage. Please address to:- The John Metcalfe Publishing Trust, Church Road, Tylers Green, Penn, Bucks, HP10 8LN.

cut here